More Praise for *Designing for Modern L*

"Kadakia and Owens masterfully adapt the best of existing training models into their new road map for modern workplace learning. Every training professional should follow their guidance to integrate learning into the business and focus on job performance."

—**Jim and Wendy Kirkpatrick**, Co-Authors, *Kirkpatrick's Four Levels of Training Evaluation*

"This book should be on every L&D professional's shelf. Kadakia and Owens offer a clear vision for the future of learning with a balance between the big picture and how to apply the ideas to programs of all sizes."

—**Zach Rubin**, Co-Founder and CEO, Professional Book Club Guru

"Kadakia and Owens offer a practical model based on thoughtful analysis of our modern learners' reality. A must-read for the L&D professional tasked with creating engaging content, driving meaningful change, and measuring the results of behavioral transformation that can only come from true learning."

—**Grace Amos**, Talent Development, Cisco

"This is a thought-provoking and practical resource that should help learning leaders and instructional designers alike. Full of fresh ideas and a new model that will help us effectively leverage new technology and multiple learning assets to serve today's modern learners."

—**Jay Rhodes**, Former Senior Director, Global Learning and Development, BCD Travel

"This book brings a much-needed update to models that haven't evolved with today's workplace. OK-LCD addresses the social learning component and scales to include learning technology that hasn't even been invented."

—**Rich Hazeltine, CPTD**, RichIntegration.com, former Head of Tech Talent Development, Zappos.com

"This book is the perfect blend of learning theory and practical tools for L&D professionals. It sparks curiosity and creativity for our field—in short, shaping us into modern learners too."

—**Chris Eversole**, Assistant Vice President, Talent Management, Ohio National Financial Services

"Our world has changed. Learning models that worked in the past have limited relevance in our dynamic and constantly changing world. Kadakia and Owens deliver a powerful learning model that responds to work conditions that are continually evolving."

—**David Richard Moore, PhD**, Professor, Innovative Learning Design & Technology, Ohio University

Designing for Modern Learning

Beyond ADDIE and SAM

CRYSTAL KADAKIA AND LISA M.D. OWENS

atd
PRESS

ATD Press is an internationally renowned source of insightful and practical information on talent development, training, and professional development.

ATD Press
1640 King Street
Alexandria, VA 22314 USA

Ordering information: Books published by ATD Press can be purchased by visiting ATD's website at td.org/books or by calling 800.628.2783 or 703.683.8100.

Library of Congress Control Number: 2020936129

ISBN-10: 1-950496-65-1
ISBN-13: 978-1-950496-65-5
e-ISBN: 978-1-950496-66-2

ATD Press Editorial Staff
Director: Sarah Halgas
Manager: Melissa Jones
Community Manager, Senior Leaders & Executives: Ann Parker
Developmental Editor: Kathryn Stafford
Text Design: Shirley E.M. Raybuck and Kathleen Dyson
Cover Design: Rose Richey

Printed by Versa Press, East Peoria, IL

*To our husbands, Jeremy and Rich. We value your insights
and cherish your support of us while we work. And we talk about
you all the time when we're off on yet another modern
learning business trip or video conference.*

*To our many colleagues who have trusted us enough to apply our
models in your workplaces and have shared your stories
of success and ideas for ongoing evolution. We are so glad we
can all reinvent learning design together.*

Contents

Foreword

Crystal Kadakia and Lisa M.D. Owens do the learning and development field a great service in this book. Let me tell you why I think this is true. The L&D field is rapidly growing more complex. There is an increasing number of theories, models, analytical and evaluation vehicles, design and development tools, and methodologies. Learning professionals have built corporate education centers, developed and implemented a wide array of learning delivery technologies, taken steps to personalize learning activities, and provided performance consulting to assist with needs assessment and learning transfer. External learning providers are proliferating, and a dizzying array of learning resources are available on the Internet and delivered by training companies and universities.

In parallel, learning is now a top survival issue and more obvious competitive advantage for companies. And learning experts are becoming valued business partners, some in the C-suite, whose job it is to bring it all together.

In short, this is a very complex and complicated field whose contributions are increasingly key to business success.

So, both learning expertise and the need for learning is accelerating, and learning resources exist for almost any learning need. *But the resources are often not assembled in a way that supports change.* In addition, they often don't appeal to today's modern learners, who expect more accessible, social, and engaging formats. It is still true, for example, that in many companies the classroom—real or virtual—is the main delivery mode for learning programs, and they are often one-and-done or one-size-fits-all solutions. The ROI from learning is often unclear and sometimes disappointing, and it is still difficult to make learning's business case to leaders or to carry learning through to real action on the job.

What Lisa and Crystal do in this book and with their model is provide a framework that helps learning professionals address these challenges and manage this increasingly complex and strategically important talent development arena. Their model makes it easier to identify and combine the best learning resources to achieve business results. And it does this while helping you personalize and modernize learning for the people who can benefit from it.

Here is the scenario that their approach will help you bring about:

> Imagine that everyone in your organization is surrounded by a curated variety of social, formal, and immediate learning resources—a learning cluster of resources (assets) that are directly targeted to building specific capabilities that are clearly related to personal and business success.

Imagine that the assets in these learning clusters range from the traditional (courses, books, learning groups, job aids) to the technology-based (video, virtual reality, apps, virtual meetings). And these clusters always include a mix of social, immediate, and formal activities that are selected by the learner based on their needs and wants. These assets include newly designed resources, as well as what's currently in your inventory or are available in the workplace, either in its original form or updated for the modern learner. In other words, new assets join with existing resources, resulting in a longer life for older assets. Everybody's learning—formal or informal—happens in a rich learner-centered environment.

The learners are surrounded by reconfigurable resources that were curated to help specific mission-critical personas achieve a strategic performance objective. It's a scenario that can triumph over the one-and-done, one-size-fits all approach to any company's learning.

The framework behind this scenario is the Owens-Kadakia Learning Cluster Design Model (OK-LCD for short). It presents an intriguing, practical, and systemic approach to organization and personal development through designed and curated learning. It's a simple model (five action-focused elements) to use deliberately and systematically, but not rigidly: the authors recognize the need for judgment and flexibility as you implement it. The model's five actions are:

- **Change.** Focus on real behavior change and results.
- **Learn.** Create personas to accommodate learner differences that relate to the objective.
- **Upgrade.** Modernize existing learning assets.
- **Surround.** Empower the learner with a meaningful learning cluster.
- **Track.** Strategically communicate transformation, not just usage.

One thing that I appreciate is that Lisa and Crystal reference and integrate others' ideas, building some of them into the details of their model (such as design thinking, Agile, and moments of learning need). Integration is a pattern that takes other forms in this book. For example, their learning clusters integrate all three categories of the 70-20-10 picture of how people learn (through daily experience, socially, and in formal learning situations). The authors also integrate learner choice and promote a view of measures that supports the collective impact of multiple assets and users. In the OK-LCD world, it's true that measures are for validation and continuous improvement. But there is also a big emphasis on using measures for communicating and marketing, as well as drawing learners into learning clusters. In other words, the authors' tendency is toward "both-and" rather than "either-or" thinking.

Lisa and Crystal are both engineers as well as learning professionals. So, what you get in this book is an analytical rigor tempered by a deep commitment to the human side (another "both-and"). You see this in the visual presentation of their OK-LCD model, which is teardrop-shaped incorporating a Venn diagram where parts overlap. Their writing has an engineer's precision, with clear and reliable chapter structures, and worksheets and diagrams to guide (assemble) the actions they propose. And they introduce some new terms that they believe add precision and signal us to wake up to a new idea or nuance.

But the book isn't a lifeless, jargon-filled manual. The authors draw you in using energizing language and stories that show their model in use.

At the beginning of this foreword, I said that Lisa and Crystal have done a great service to the field. The crux of that service is that they provide a new way to organize formal, on-the-job, and social learning into learning clusters that are tailored for the business and the modern learners who will experience them. Their framework addresses the full cycle of learning design, from the articulation of terminal and instrumental goals through to evaluating and communicating impact. It's also a no waste approach that provides a guide for updating and modernizing existing resources as well as adding new ones, including new technologies when they are fit for purpose. Worksheets and guidance in the book support a rigorous and rational approach to learning design. But the advanced learning professional will find plenty of space to improvise.

This book triggered many ideas for my work to help people to become smarter, more self-transforming learners and to build learning enterprises. I am sure you will find immense value for your own work—both as you learn about and implement the OK-LCD model and as it inspires your creative actions in this fast-transforming field.

Patricia A. McLagan
Organization Transformation Advisor and
Author, *Unstoppable You: Adopt the New
Learning 4.0 Mindset and Change Your Life*

Preface

A New Strategy for L&D

What would motivate two individuals to come together to write a book on modernizing learning? Two people whose key roles in life have been intertwined in the art of learning design. We both love learning, and even more so, we both love helping people connect the dots to have their own aha moments. This book is for those like us who are passionate about helping people grow and are constantly expanding their own thinking and skills at doing so. We like living and exploring at the edge, and we hope our readers do too.

We, like many others, have been waiting for this moment in learning and development. Businesses are focused on L&D more than ever to upskill the workforce as roles change rapidly and become more complex. Employees and new hires are demanding learning and development opportunities. Plus, there are all the new ways L&D can create and facilitate high-quality capability building through technology. We've seen the training industry evolve from sage on the stage style to more democratic and learner-centered styles. Yet, we've noticed that L&D hasn't quite made the leap into the modern digital age.

What's holding us back? Is it cost or time? Or perhaps turf wars between L&D, HR, IT, or other internal silos?

We think it's something more fundamental. We believe that L&D's job is changing and to leverage this moment in time, L&D will have to shift strategies. We are confident that the strategies in this book will help the L&D industry emerge as a key contributor to the business's success and as heroes to its employees. We also believe that it is you, our partners staying at the cutting-edge of L&D, who will make this happen.

The New Job of L&D

When we were challenged in 2015, to describe how to meet the needs of modern learners, we dug into learning research and uncovered the common L&D issues of the day. They all pointed toward a need for a fundamental change in what we see as our goal and how we get there. Our biggest insight was realizing that the instructional design industry was singularly focused on designing one thing—an L&D deliverable that would close the capability gap. It might take the form of a classroom training program, an e-learning course, learning program, or a manual, but it is still just one element. Of course, L&D often adds in a job aid or a link to additional content, but there isn't enough strategic thinking behind such additions. Our traditional and current instructional design models—such as ADDIE, SAM, Agile, and even design thinking—all inherently assume that the job of L&D is to create a single main deliverable.

We learned other things we weren't expecting. For example, the L&D industry is trying to meet today's needs using antiquated models and tools. Sure, they're great tools, but they're also three and four decades old! Even the changes L&D has adopted more recently—like CD-ROM training, web-based and virtual training, and blended learning—are just incremental modifications when compared to the technology-driven changes occurring in the world around us. While we access technology at home as reflexively as taking a breath, learning at work is far more out of reach. We are living in the middle of a revolution of disruptive innovation, and L&D needs to be an integral part of that movement.

Slowly, we started to see a new answer take shape. Modern learners want to be able to choose how, when, and where they want and need to learn. Therefore, L&D's new goal is to develop and deliver a learning cluster to replace the single-minded focus on one training deliverable per skill. A learning cluster is what we call it when L&D strategically designs and develops a set of learning assets to help learners gain a capability. This is what L&D needs to be able to do to level up for living, working, and learning in a digital world. It puts learning at a person's fingertips in a high-quality, personalized way. We in L&D need to use the available technology, but we have to do it intentionally, choicefully, and systematically.

With this approach comes a new language and a new way to talk about the products L&D creates. We'll deliver learning clusters instead of a class. We'll design learning assets instead of a learning session. We'll produce learning products that are available at various touchpoints for our learners, not just in the classroom or on the online training portal.

We shared this concept in workshops for several years. The learning cluster was very well received by participants, who then readily shared their own experiences as they developed learning clusters where they work. As usual, the teacher learns as much as the student.

The learning cluster evolved into the Owens-Kadakia Learning Cluster Design (OK-LCD) model. *Designing for Modern Learning: Beyond ADDIE and SAM* is a culmination of the knowledge we gained on this journey to provide a new strategy for L&D that works for modern learners and their businesses. We wrote it because we want to share our work with a broader audience. In this book, we'll show you how the OK-LCD strategy, model, and tools enable designs using your learning content that work and are scalable for the exponentially changing future.

Your Road Map to the Book

There needs to be a model or plan to guide L&D. We've developed that plan—the Owens-Kadakia Learning Cluster Design model—and we describe its iterative process in the next nine chapters.

Chapter 1 explains why L&D needs to, as we say, "join the revolution." It helps describe what training professionals rarely have the time to consider—what has shifted in our world and what that means for us in L&D. Chapter 2 introduces a high-level view of a strategic solution for L&D—the OK-LCD model. We share that the OK-LCD model is both a new way of thinking and a new way of doing. We also explain the new way of a thinking for L&D.

Then in chapters 3 through 7, we dig into the model and how it works—by going through each of the five L&D Actions that make up the model. We tell a common L&D story that continues throughout these chapters and features the perspective of business leaders, L&D professionals, and learners. The story reveals current and common frustrations, while showing how application of the OK-LCD model can make a difference. Then we explain what the Action is all about and provide details about how to do it using a tool we've created for each Action.

We're also very proud of the "In Practice" sections featured in these chapters. These are real stories from real people who have adopted our model. We cover a diverse range of organizations, including the Gorilla Glue Company, Visa, and Bluescape. Not only are the results they've achieved incredible, but we know you'll learn a lot from reading about the real-life process to get there.

We also gathered what we've learned and pulled together a start-to-finish fictional example, which you'll see in chapter 8. It shows how each Action works together to create something bigger and shares the kinds of conversations L&D will have while implementing the OK-LCD model.

Finally, chapter 9 is about the future of L&D with the OK-LCD model. It describes the wins the telecommunications company Comcast has achieved by doing so much that aligns directly with the OK-LCD model. We also describe the barriers to getting to that future L&D state, and how to move through those barriers. We end the chapter by designing and presenting our own learning cluster for the OK-LCD model. Use it to guide your learning when, where, and however you want to learn.

You can read this book by starting at the beginning and reading through to the end, or you can choose your own path. Maybe you just want to read the first two chapters, then skim all the stories and examples. Or you might want to start with the tools at the end in the Appendix and then read the "The Action Implemented" sections, followed by the chapter 8 case study. Or maybe you prefer just reading the theory parts in chapters 1 and 2 and the "The Action Explained" sections in chapters 3–7. It's up to you. The point is, we've modeled what we preach. You have the option to learn when, where, and how you want. The headings and layout is designed to help you easily navigate the book to find what interests you most. Or if you want to do a deep dive, go grab your coffee and get immersed!

But the end is not the end. Learning is an ongoing thing. Living at the edge of L&D lasts a lifetime. So, we provide an appendix with our current tools for the model's five L&D Actions. And we provide support for bringing learning clusters to life through our ongoing work, which you can learn more about at LearningClusterDesign.com. There, we encourage you to join the community, get the latest templates, seek expert help for using the model, and share what you learn. When we write the next edition of the book, we hope to fill it with new stories and new insights from our readers as our model spreads and shapes the future of the L&D industry.

Welcome to *Designing for Modern Learning: Beyond ADDIE and SAM*. We're glad to have you join us on this revolutionary journey!

1

Mapping the Past and Present for the Future

modern learning is continuous, on the spot, craved, a part of everyday conversation, two-way, crowdsourced, contextual, and vital. When we ask people today about their relationship with learning—young, old, in the workforce, in school, at home—we find that learning is no longer a luxury to be indulged in at particular stages of life or career. Whether or not their employer or circumstance supports it, people crave remaining relevant, solving in-the-moment problems, and having the opportunity to learn whenever and wherever they need it. Now, with the advent of digital technology, this need, this zeal for lifelong learning, is as close as one's fingertips. People often talk about the recent podcast they heard or a new how-to video they watched when they needed to solve a problem. They contribute to the pool of knowledge by adding their own content. The introduction of digital technology grew the possibility, necessity, and hunger for lifelong learning.

In comparison, training is event-based, obligatory, one and done, top-down controlled, out of context, outdated, and scheduled.

While training and development professionals are the learning experts, it's quickly becoming apparent that our systems, history, and process enable us to be experts in only limited avenues of learning: primarily classroom and programmatic methods. As a result, the deliverables produced by our training departments are used infrequently, and the training department's resources are not the first, second, or third stop on an employee's journey to learning. According to Degreed's 2016 study of the anthropology behind how the workforce learns, employees are finding ways to learn weekly or even daily. Yet they use L&D-provided training, on average, only once a quarter.

Consider our industry's typical approach and imagine the resulting perception by employees and by the business:

- We ask employees to learn on a schedule set by us.
- We take orders from our customers and leaders, often placing the highest priority on topics necessary to mitigate business risk.
- We often fail to voice our observations of what's needed for higher performance or for the future of the business.
- We don't focus on learner support outside the program.
- We create training and request content only from those we deem subject matter experts.

The resulting perception? All too often, training departments are seen as unable to meet the needs of digital-age learners and businesses. We lack the capability, philosophy, and process to pull together the optimal diversity of learning assets to meet the needs of the modern workforce we serve (Figure 1-1).

Figure 1-1. Two Contrasting Approaches: Traditional Training and Modern Learning

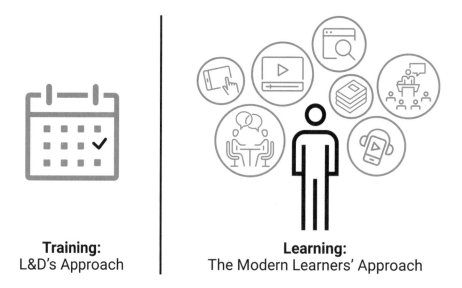

Training:
L&D's Approach

Learning:
The Modern Learners' Approach

The world has changed, and while our existing instructional design models have helped us in the past, it's time for a new model to catch up to the here and now of learning. Without understanding the shifts in learning and business that have taken place, L&D professionals run the risk of being sidelined, unable or powerless to guide our organizations through the complexities and opportunities of the virtual age.

In this chapter, we describe the numerous, seismic shifts in learners' realities and the transformations in structure and profitability that are revolutionizing our business organizations. We then consider the evolution of our L&D profession as we respond to our changing world.

Let's start by exploring a common story that is repeating itself today, in many forms, across our industry in companies and organizations. We'll revisit the organization in this story throughout the book. These stories reflect the issues L&D faces when using common approaches to designing learning. In later chapters, you will find some contrasting stories that highlight how reality shifts with our new model.

A Common L&D Story

Cast of Characters:

CEO
Doug

CMO
Raj

CHRO
Chris

The Scene: Doug and Raj are having one of their regular meetings.

"Raj, I agree that we have to take on this upgrade you're proposing if we're going to be successful with these new players," said Doug, CEO of the company, to the CMO. "But how can we build employee skills quickly enough to accommodate the change? One of my biggest headaches these days is finding and keeping employees to do the work, and then training them sufficiently to do the job right."

"I hear you, Doug," Raj said. "Hiring talent is harder than ever, and even experienced hires seem to need additional training to do their job. Heck, it takes three days just to get them out of the new hire training. Then, once we teach them how to do the job, they need more training to stay up to speed on the latest products and business systems."

Talent development was a challenge becoming all too familiar to the CEO.

"And what do we get for all this training?" Doug countered. "Chris tells me that employees like the training, and she has the numbers to prove it. But I'm not sure that all the training is making any difference. For one, I don't care if they like it or not; I just want them to be able to do the job. Further, I just read the summary of exit interviews for the last fiscal. One of the top complaints, right after 'I should be promoted,' was that more than 60 percent said, 'Provide more training and development opportunities.' So, despite a 10 percent bump up in staffing for the training department, and a big increase for the new training software, employees continue to say they aren't getting enough training and development."

"But do the employees even take the training?" Raj wondered aloud. "Everyone I talk to is way too busy to take any training. It's a big deal when someone takes two days off to attend a course. A few people have said they like the webinar trainings because they can multitask during the course."

Doug gave a wry grin. "Well, that sounds very educational! So, what are we getting for our investment in training? I'm reading in *Harvard Business Review* about leaders being the teachers and about success with peer-to-peer learning. Maybe that's the answer: Cut out the middleman; cut out L&D for everything but compliance and employee onboarding."

Raj nodded in agreement with his CEO. "I've been reading about virtual reality training and algorithms that can tell just what an employee needs to know. Maybe we should be investing in a more modern learning organization," he suggested. "Or maybe we should give the job to someone in the IT department. At least they can connect their spending to some type of ROI."

The Issues:
- Is L&D becoming irrelevant to the business? How can we change that?
- Should we eliminate L&D and move to a different learning model, such as peer-to-peer learning or leaders as teachers?
- How can we upskill employees quickly to achieve our company goals?
- How can L&D organizations deal with requests for even more training?

Shifts in Learning

We all often discuss the Internet, computers, and mobile devices and remark on how things have changed dramatically. But what exactly has changed, and what is the impact these changes have on learning? Historically, prior to digital technology, learning was presented in written form (textbooks, job aids) and, after the invention of the television, in one-way video. It took time to create learning materials in these formats, and not everyone had the capability or availability to do so. Traditional instructional design models were made for this historical world—and its limitations. Training departments' customers—the learners and the business—aligned their expectations to the same limitations of that time.

Digital technology has changed the face of training delivery and use. While L&D people tell us that they feel the shift, we all struggle to articulate just what has happened and how to react. Yet, identifying what shifted is the first step in formulating a strategic response. That is what we set out to do. This chapter describes the four shifts we have identified. The next chapter is a helicopter view of the strategic response we formulated in the Owens-Kadakia Learning Cluster Design (OK-LCD) model. The four primary shifts are:
- when and where learning happens
- who creates and delivers training
- how we find information
- how we ensure information is reliable.

When and Where Learning Happens

In the not-too-distant past, individuals had three primary ways to learn. They could read a physical book anywhere, anytime; locate an expert to guide them; or find an in-person class. The learning options were quite limited. Today, digital technology allows people to learn whenever and wherever they are, with increasingly sophisticated tools that more fully mimic the classroom experience. Especially with advances in areas such as virtual and augmented reality, immersive learning experiences can and are being designed for both technical and soft skills. (For more on virtual reality and future tech examples, see chapters 6 and 9, respectively.)

Who Creates and Delivers Learning

Once upon a time, the barriers to sharing knowledge were high. Experts had to be found and approved before they would be given the opportunity to author content or teach a course. The tools to create content were costly and available only to specialized businesses, such as publishers, or to internal functions that chose to pursue media creation. Today, digital technology allows anyone to create content using the ubiquitous smartphone, and to converse with whomever they deem an expert, not just those selected by their organization as subject matter expert. Crowdsourcing content is acceptable, if not encouraged and expected.

How We Find Information

There was a time when employees had no choice of where to go for information. To learn something new, they went through their training departments and a few course catalogs, or they attended conferences provided by professional associations. They searched libraries via the card catalog, and were dependent on whatever was available there. The knowledge pool was limited, so the demand for learning materials was naturally high. Today, with powerful search engines, a global network of content and content providers, and advances in artificial intelligence (AI), employees have a lot of options that are sorted and filtered for them instantaneously. (For more on AI, see chapter 5.)

How We Ensure Information Is Reliable

With lower barriers to who creates content, the possibility of misinformation increases. Today, we all rely on the crowd to tell us what's good and what's not. Rather than trusting media creators to present us with experts, we rely on one another to filter and review data. While this can initially sound risky, with more and different voices, our social systems reflect more diverse thinking and less biased points of view.

Each of these four shifts creates new expectations for learning opportunities. The shift in when, where, and how we find information leads people to expect continuous, contextual learning. The shift in how we ensure that information is reliable drives an expectation for learning to be two-way and crowdsourced. Where learning was once limited by time, space, and resources, today we expect it to be at our fingertips.

Shifts in Business

Digital technology hasn't changed expectations only in learning and development. It has also been hard at work transforming organization structure and profitability. Systems rooted in the industrial age were shaken by new and disruptive business models made possible in the digital age. To remain viable, businesses are adapting to the following four key environmental shifts, creating new demands on their talent:

- exponential rate of change
- when and where work gets done
- demographic shifts
- types of work.

Exponential Rate of Change

Moore's Law, an observation by Gordon Moore that the number of transistors on a chip would double while costs halve every two years, drove the last 50 years of exponential technology change. While there is debate whether this trend will continue, there is no question that new technologies will persist in disrupting and transforming life as we know it. Business leaders have the tough task of adapting their organizations to the latest change while keeping a keen eye on what the future might hold. Business as usual is no longer an adequate strategy.

When and Where Work Gets Done

Similar to the anytime, anywhere possibility of learning, work is more than ever on the go. No longer limited to the assembly line, work and profit are tied to more cognitive and relational work. According to a 2019 survey by the International Workplace Group, 70 percent of employees work at least one day a week somewhere other than the office, and more than half work remotely at least half of the week. And businesses report that flexible working strategies increase business growth, competitiveness, productivity, and the ability to attract and retain top talent. A two-year study published in the *Quarterly Journal of Economics* verified that there was an impressive increase in work productivity among people who worked from home (Bloom et al. 2015). This affects HR policies, including pay, performance management, hiring and firing, and of course, how people learn. Work is more global and mobile than ever.

Demographic Shifts

The workplace is experiencing a massive demographic shift. Experienced talent is aging—either retiring and taking their capability with them or staying on the job and requiring new or updated skills to stay relevant. New talent is entering the scene, with Generation Z (born between 1995 and 2015) expected to make up an ever-growing part of the workforce by 2025. Given the talent pool's dramatically different digital technology experiences, leaders and managers cannot expect employees to carry the same understanding of values, etiquette, motivations, and thought processes. Amid these differences, organizations must consider how to transfer knowledge effectively across all generations.

Type of Work

A Deloitte study showed that how companies generate profit has shifted from activities related to tangible goods and equipment to activities related to intangible services, cognition, and insight (Benko, Gorman, and Steinberg 2014). When the type of work changes, so do the types of employees, the organizational structure we place them in, and the tools and training we provide. Organizations regularly compete for employees with desirable, complex skill sets. Now, even the information economy is transitioning to the human economy. With the routine and highly analytical tasks people do today being done better and more accurately by robotics and AI, talent is shifting their types of work to contribute differently in a world of technology. Here is how Dov Seidman (2014) described it:

> In the human economy, the most valuable workers will be hired hearts. The know-how and analytic skills that made them indispensable in the knowledge economy no longer give them an advantage over increasingly intelligent machines. But they will still bring to their work essential traits that can't be and won't be programmed into software, like creativity, passion, character, and collaborative spirit—their humanity, in other words. The ability to leverage these strengths will be the source of one organization's superiority over another.

The output needed from talent in the industrial age was focused on efficiency, repeatability, and tasks. As a result of the shifts of the digital age, organizations need talent to have new capabilities:

- Reskill or upgrade at the pace of innovation.
- Demonstrate soft skills that work virtually and across demographic or regional boundaries.
- Handle more complex, ambiguous tasks.

These four shifts for the business also affect L&D professionals—our purpose, our products, and our own skill sets (Figure 1-2).

Figure 1-2. How Will L&D Evolve?

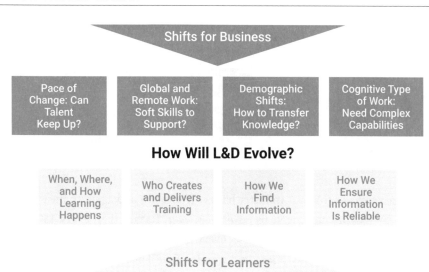

Where once they produced training for job onboarding to improve time to productivity, compliance training to avoid business risk, or technical and job-related training critical for business operation, today the business has new, emerging learning needs. But because these new needs are things that training departments did not historically do, many businesses do not realize that L&D can do them, and do them well! We are the learning experts, and we must and can step up to fill these gaps in this new world. If our businesses and our learners have to adapt, what's stopping us from adapting to these shifts?

Trial and Error: L&D's Attempts at Evolution

Our industry has a history of listening to the business need and adapting. Like businesses of the industrial age, training is a very structured field, designed for efficiency. It's in our culture and goes back to our historical roots. The training industry emerged during and after World War II in a time of expanding technological innovation, a period of collaboration between industry and the U.S. War Manpower Commission. The goal was to produce military equipment as fast as possible by upskilling a high volume of workers efficiently. Later, instructional design models were established to help provide structure and consistency to what had been an amorphous, unreliable process. Learning was based in the classroom or on the job. Since then, although contexts for learning have changed, our instructional design models have struggled to help create rigor and quality experiences in this new world—where content changes faster than training can be generated. Take a look at the infographic on the evolution of talent development (Figure 1-3).

Figure 1-3. The Evolution of Talent Development

The infographic shows us that our industry has evolved again and again to meet the current needs. It also shows how changes are coming at us faster than ever. Rather than every 150 or even 48 years, we are now making a dramatic shift, on average, every five years. It's no surprise that many of us rate ourselves as 10 or 20 years behind the times—and wonder if we'll ever catch up.

In our work and collaboration with companies, we've observed three strategies training departments employ in reaction to the changes of the digital age (Figure 1-4).

Figure 1-4. Three Common L&D Strategies in Reaction to the Digital Age

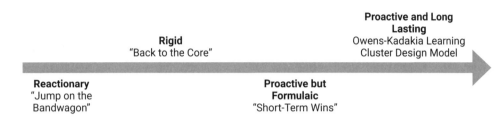

Strategy 1: Reactionary

It can be argued that reactionary means not having a strategy at all, and in fact, this is what we see with some training departments. Overwhelmed by the changes, these departments invest in the latest technologies, directed by alluring whitepapers, conferences, and quick comparisons to leading companies. Often, these investments are sold as a business case, but are not thought through from an implementation standpoint. Employee usage never quite takes off. Doing what's sexy in the moment leads to an anxiety-filled, unsuccessful training department.

Strategy 2: Rigid

Some training departments become more insular in the face of these changes. Their motto is "Let's get back to our core expertise." To maintain relevance, they feel that honing their existing skills is where they can and will continue to add value to their organizations. These training departments continue to be treated as order takers while the business looks to other sources to meet its talent development needs. Their deliverables continue to solely take the form of classroom instruction, manuals, job aids, and, grudgingly, e-learning.

Strategy 3: Proactive, but Formulaic

The last strategy holds the most promise, but still falls short. In this strategy, training departments are using new prescriptive models based on the latest thought leadership. Unfortunately, most of these new models are still focused on telling designers what to create, often through formulaic approaches. Prescriptions for e-learning design, bite-size learning, blended learning, and the overall mix of learning might meet an immediate need, but leave the organization vulnerable to future changes.

An L&D Strategy for the Next 100 Years

You are likely familiar with the three strategies we've described and are even able to place your own L&D organization on the scale. The training industry, encumbered by fear of a significantly different era or a desire for quick wins, struggles to find an approach to evolve strategically. Is there a strategy that can help training departments effectively evolve in light of these changes? An approach that can serve as a long-lasting foundation for designing learning for the next 100 years? We believe there is a fourth approach: a proactive, process-based, long-lasting philosophy. We believe the Owens-Kadakia Learning Cluster Design (OK-LCD) model is the answer. The OK-LCD model is both a philosophy and a process. In this philosophy, we don't focus on telling L&D "what" to create for a digital age; we focus on building capability around the thought process—the "how" and "why" for a digital age. OK-LCD encourages rigor coupled with a mentality at the speed of business. We start by removing the limiting assumptions we've historically made in the industrial age and work with the reality of what training can do today.

Before and After: A Modern L&D Organization

Our organizations are desperately looking for help. The *2017 Deloitte Global Human Capital Trends* report shared that 70 percent of CEOs say their organizations do not have the skills to adapt to today's environment, and 42 percent of Millennials say they are likely to leave their organization because they are not learning fast enough. Yet CEOs are not experts at evaluating skills gaps and crafting learning. They are waiting for someone—an expert—to tell them what needs to be done in this tough reality. Frustratingly, in the *2017 LinkedIn Workplace Learning Report*, fewer than a quarter of L&D professionals were willing to recommend their own L&D organization to peers. When L&D serves as order takers, we assume someone else is a greater expert than us at learning! But why would finance, marketing, engineering, or operations leaders be able to perform this role better than we can?

If we in L&D change the way we approach our job, what is possible for the future of L&D? Imagine a future L&D that collaborates with leadership and other talent development functions to determine the most business-critical capability needs as being the norm across the industry. In these strategic conversations, the future L&D owns and can articulate the highly valuable data on what employees have been motivated to learn so far and where progress has been slow. The future L&D is not seen only as a resource to mitigate business risks through training, but as the vehicle and leader in meeting the business needs and creating a learning culture.

From an employee point of view, this future L&D is on top of the latest technologies, but more important, uses historic L&D expertise to structure learning experiences. Rather than receiving random information through a frustrating smorgasbord of technologies that is tough to navigate and hard to find, employees know that L&D has made sure that there are easy-to-find, meaningful ways to grow their capability. This future L&D is a seamless supporter of their ability to perform on the job. When they need something, they use the L&D-provided avenues to find it.

Final Notes

"Learning is an experience. Everything else is just information." —Albert Einstein

The training industry has evolved over time, but the pace of change is increasing, just as it is for our learners and businesses. The future of L&D in a digital age is about unleashing human potential rather than reinforcing quality, routine work. To date, the strategies to evolve have been insufficient to help the majority of L&D. However, by identifying the primary shifts for learning and business, L&D could be a central, vital capability for the organization—if we choose to evolve and move past our own resistance to change. L&D is being called to a higher level of service and capability. Will you answer that call? To learn how, let's continue to the next chapter, where we introduce the Owens-Kadakia Learning Cluster Design Model.

Reflect

◊ How have you witnessed the shifts in learning? Shifts in business? What impact have these shifts had on your training organization?

◊ Looking at Figure 1-4, where would you place your organization on the training industry strategy spectrum? Why?

◊ How would you like to see L&D serve the organization in the future? If you consider your wildest dreams, what do you envision as L&D's role?

2

Adopting a New Model for Our Changing World

Why do we in L&D need a new model? The expectations and realities have dramatically changed since our current instructional design (ID) models gained wide use. These models simply were never intended to deal with today's complexities. The Owens-Kadakia Learning Cluster Design model deals with these shifts, changes, and complexities. As you read this chapter on the OK-LCD model, form your own opinion about the answers to these questions:

- How might the OK-LCD principles make a difference for me? For the L&D industry?
- The model asks L&D to adopt new actions. What will it take to do so?
- How does the model support the next evolution for L&D?

What Is It? The Owens-Kadakia Learning Cluster Design Model

We developed the model in response to the question, "How should we be designing for modern learning?" This model, developed and iterated over the past five years, is grounded in the fields of instructional systems development, neuroscience, cognitive and developmental psychology, and organization development. Throughout this book, you will read the stories of early practitioners of the OK-LCD model.

In this chapter, we introduce the model and describe the four principles behind the model, five Actions that make up the model, and the defining characteristics of OK-LCD. We will also discuss how the model works in harmony with other models, as well as the learning theories that ground our approach.

The OK-LCD Model

The OK-LCD model is composed of five Actions for L&D professionals to take when designing modern learning (Figure 2-1). The model represents the holistic answer to many of our current L&D challenges and was developed by:

- questioning the past, specifically the assumptions about the goals and process of L&D work that were established in pre-digital times
- considering the present shifts learners and businesses are experiencing
- reviewing the latest in neuroscience and learning theory
- reflecting on our experiences and those of our OK-LCD workshop participants.

Figure 2-1. The OK-LCD Model

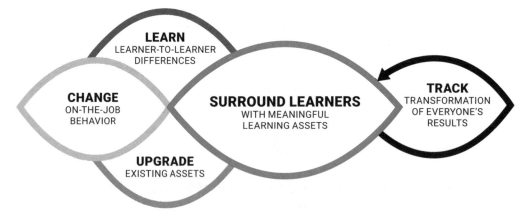

The model is unique in that it embodies a philosophy—a way of thinking—and a process of step-by-step actions. At its essence, the OK-LCD model is an intentional, context-centered approach to selecting, designing, and facilitating access to a set of learning assets to improve performance on the job for a particular capability in today's digital age.

This is a change for both your job and your goals in L&D. Because learners have more tools available to learn, and businesses need more complex capability from talent faster than ever, L&D needs to shift our focus. Instead of designing one training program per capability gap, L&D needs to shift to designing multiple assets and connecting learners with the learning assets they need. This is what designing modern learning means, and it is the heart of the OK-LCD approach.

First, let's get familiar with new terminology and the principles behind the model.

A New Language

The following terms were developed as part of our work on the OK-LCD model and will be used throughout the book:

- **Modern Learner:** someone who needs to learn fast in an ever-changing environment, and who will access a wide variety of resources to get answers.
- **Learning Cluster:** a set of learning assets intended to address a specific performance gap across multiple contexts, which we call learning touchpoints.
- **Learning Asset:** a very general term describing a wide range of things that help people learn. It might be content to read, an online search, a class (face-to-face or online), a discussion, a video, or even a motivational poster. It can be as small as a 30-second audio recording or as large as a three-month class. In traditional training, a learning asset most often takes the form of a class, an e-learning course, or a blended learning program.
- **Learning Touchpoints:** the points of contact between modern learners and how they get the learning they need in the way that they need it to succeed in their work. These can be tagged as having characteristics that are social, formal, and immediate.
- **OK-LCD Action:** describes an L&D activity and responsibility as a part of engaging in the OK-LCD model for modern learning design.

Our language can help us drive change or keep us in the past. We encourage you to adopt a modern way of speaking, using terms that are part of the OK-LCD model and principles.

The Principles of the OK-LCD Model

First and foremost, the OK-LCD model calls for a new way of thinking, a new understanding about L&D's goal and role in organizations (Figure 2-2). The five Actions we created reflect a philosophy captured in these four principles:

1. **Go beyond one-and-done.** L&D's new role is to deliver and facilitate access to multiple learning assets to build employee capability. It's no longer sufficient for L&D to design one learning asset—a class or course—to meet a business's or an employee's learning goal.
2. **Design the whole, not the parts.** Multiple learning assets must be viewed and designed as part of an integrated whole (what we have coined the "learning cluster"), both as part of L&D's design and from the learner point of view. These multiple assets cannot be effective if they're created ad hoc.
3. **Focus on learner needs.** Our context as training designers and deliverers is no longer as important as the context of the learner. Whereas in the past L&D had limited tools to deliver

learning, today we can deliver learning when, where, and how the learner needs it. L&D must reflect a deeper understanding of the learner and the capability gap first.

4. **Change on-the-job behavior.** L&D can and should be held accountable for improving performance on the job, not just at the end of a training class, course, or program. Improved performance means that there will be a change in behavior through application on the job, rather than simply acquiring the knowledge and skill during the program.

Figure 2-2. OK-LCD Model's Philosophy: L&D's New Job

Here's the difference between our past philosophies and this modern one: If you approach a learning project as designing training and enabling knowledge acquisition, then you are living by time-honored, traditional instructional development principles and assumptions. However, if instead you approach a learning project as designing and facilitating access to a wide variety of learning assets, and as empowering and measuring behavior change in the workplace, then you are living by the principles embedded in the Owens-Kadakia Learning Cluster Design model—and you are seamlessly connecting learners with the resources they need to change behavior on the job to deliver the desired business results.

We encourage you to use the Actions and the associated Tools, but at a minimum, we hope you are inspired to adopt the philosophy and principles behind OK-LCD as you bring your L&D work into the digital age.

OK-LCD's Five Actions

OK-LCD is more than a philosophy. The model is a set of Actions that tell L&D how to create a new product. Instead of focusing on designing just one class or course to address skills gaps, with OK-LCD, we create learning clusters. To create learning clusters, the model takes L&D practitioners through five Actions. The Action names create a memorable mnemonic: CLUSTER. Here is a brief overview of each Action:

- **C: Change on-the-job behavior.** In the Change Action, set the goal for the learning cluster (called a strategic performance objective). This goal articulates the connection between learners' on-the-job performance and the desired business results. This is one of three early Actions leading to the Surround Action.
- **L: Learn learner-to-learner differences.** In the Learn Action, identify learner personas within the target learner group whose behavior change will have the greatest effect on the desired business impact. Persona definitions go beyond demographics and job type to explore contexts of when, where, and how each persona will most likely need to learn. This Action guides strategic choices in the Surround Action.
- **U: Upgrade existing assets.** In the Upgrade Action, apply the nine elements of modern learning to quickly improve current programs. As a bonus, the ideas for new learning assets identified here will jump-start the work in the Surround Action.
- **S: Surround learners with meaningful assets.** In the Surround Action, combine the work and insights from the other Actions to intentionally select learning assets across all three learning touchpoints (social, formal, immediate) to build a learning cluster that will meet the learning needs for each crucial learner persona. Taken together, these learning assets should deliver both the desired behavior change on the job and the related business results.
- **TER: Track transformation of Everyone's Results.** In the Track Action, identify those measures—qualitative and quantitative—that will indicate the impact of the learning cluster. Then track these measures and turn the results into a story about the impact of learning. Use the results for further improvements.

To make it easier to talk about these Actions in day-to-day conversation and in our OK-LCD workshops, we use abbreviated names that you will see throughout this book. We say the "Change Action," the "Learn Action," and so forth. In the coming chapters, you will read complete descriptions of each Action, how to use the associated Tools to implement the Action, and the impact that typically results.

OK-LCD's Defining Characteristics

"The more compatible the theory and philosophy are to the context in which a model is to be applied, the greater the potential that the original intent of the model will be achieved." —Gustafson and Branch (2002)

We believe that the OK-LCD model is more compatible with our current context of learning and working within a volatile, uncertain, complex, and ambiguous (VUCA) world. As such, the model has greater potential to help learning professionals make a bigger impact with modern learning design.

Every model is unique and has a few defining characteristics. Here are a few things to keep in mind as you apply the OK-LCD model:

- **Actions.** This model is not a simple checklist of steps or stages. Rather, with this model, L&D needs to purposefully act to shift into the future. While the OK-LCD model shows a logical sequence for the Actions from left to right, you can begin with any Action, because they all build upon one another. We encourage you to simply get started, and then make sure to cover each Action from there. Your starting point should align with your needs and context. Then, as you thoughtfully fulfill the purpose of that Action, you will progress to other actions.
- **Incrementally iterative.** The model's Actions are not necessarily one-and-done. The thought process within each Action continuously references the goals and activities of other Actions. At times, this influences, or even changes, the other Actions during the project. Don't think of it as having to "go back and fix something." Think of it in the same way as the SAM (Successive Approximation Model) or Agile approach. With each iteration, the entire learning cluster improves!
- **Centered on learning clusters.** The Surround Learners With Meaningful Assets Action is the heart of the model. In the Surround Action, we design the learning cluster. All other Actions contribute to, and gain feedback from, the learning cluster. For example, the Learn Action helps you brainstorm the types of learning assets that are most relevant for each persona within their unique moments of learning need.
- **Tools.** Each Action has an associated Tool to guide your thinking as you generate outputs or deliverables. You'll get a brief overview of each Tool in the chapters on that Action. Then, in chapter 8 you will see a start-to-finish case study of what it is like to design a learning cluster using the Tools. Further, in the appendix, you will get a copy of these tools, with detailed instructions on how to use them built right in. You can get the latest version of the Tools at LearningClusterDesign.com/Book-Bonus.
- **Ongoing community.** For further support and learning, we encourage you to explore LearningClusterDesign.com. Here, you can download the most up-to-date Tools and stay fresh with our latest research and in-practice case studies. You can also explore other learning assets to continue to grow your capability in the model. This is our way of practicing what we preach, by giving you a variety of strategically chosen ways, times, and places to upskill in the model.

What's Included? Tapping Into Proven Learning Frameworks and Models

Three models are so integral to the thinking and execution of OK-LCD that we want to provide you with a basic description. These are Bob Mosher and Conrad Gottfredson's Five Moments of Learning Need (2011), Kirkpatrick's Four Levels of Evaluation, and the AGES model, which came out of the NeuroLeadership Institute (Davachi et al. 2010). As you go through the remainder of the book, keep these learning theories in mind to help you understand the connection between each Action and how it facilitates learning.

Five Moments of Learning Need

In 2011, Mosher and Gottfredson shared their theory, the Five Moments of Learning Need. Even with the technology available a decade ago, they saw the possibility for L&D to shift our focus from delivering only formal learning to playing a role in what they call "informal intentional" learning. They noticed that traditional training wasn't enough for the pace of change everyone was experiencing. Much of learning, out of necessity, was occurring after employees had left the classroom, through what Mosher and Gottfredson call "informal independent" learning opportunities. By leveraging informal intentional learning, companies and their employees could, at a minimum, shorten time to closing capability gaps while avoiding the risks due to inaccurate informal independent learning.

To guide the design of informal intentional learning, Mosher and Gottfredson focused on delineating the situations in which employees need to learn. They called these the Moments of Learning Need, and defined them as shown (Figure 2-3).

Figure 2-3. Mosher and Gottfredson's Five Moments of Learning Need

New	More	Apply	Solve	Change
Learning something for the first time	Expanding the breadth of what has been learned	Acting upon what they have learned	Solving a problem or resolving an issue	Learning new ways of doing something and adapting

The Five Moments of Learning Need empower L&D to understand learner context—a major factor in learner-centric design. As you dive deep into the OK-LCD model, you can see how the Five Moments of Learning Need help you think through the Learn Action. And the Five Moments direct your attention to the "when" of employee learning, thus helping you provide meaningful learning assets when, where, and how your learners want and need to learn (Surround Action). Mosher and Gottfredson's work helps you think through the context of learning from your learners' perspective.

Kirkpatrick's Four Levels of Evaluation

While many people think about evaluating after the learning program is complete, L&D professionals know that we should address evaluation right from the start when designing a learning program. This helps clarify our goals so we can maximize desired on-the-job performance and organizational results. As the Kirkpatricks remind us, "When companies invest in training, they expect results." The Four Levels of Training Evaluation (Figure 2-4), are credited to Donald Kirkpatrick and his pioneering work in 1959. The model has four evaluation steps: reaction, learning, behavior, and results. Throughout the design process, we continue to loop back to the evaluation goals, resulting in interactive tweaks to the design, method of measurement, and even the goals themselves.

Figure 2-4. Kirkpatrick's Four Levels of Training Evaluation

Level 4: Results
Level 3: Behavior
Level 2: Learning
Level 1: Reaction

The Kirkpatrick model is deceptively simple and amazingly powerful when applied throughout the learning asset design, roll out, and use. The four levels are:

- **Level 1: Reaction.** The degree to which participants find the training favorable, engaging, and relevant to their jobs.
- **Level 2: Learning.** The degree to which participants acquire the intended knowledge, skills, attitude, confidence, and commitment based on their participation in the training.
- **Level 3: Behavior.** The degree to which participants apply what they've learned during training when they are back on the job.
- **Level 4: Results.** The degree to which targeted outcomes occur as a result of the training and the support and accountability package.

The AGES Model

The AGES theory helps showcase how the OK-LCD model supports learning from a neuroscience perspective (Figure 2-5). In the whitepaper *The Neuroscience of Making Learning Stick*, the authors state, "The four principles, which we term 'AGES,' summarize the big drivers of memory systems in the brain during encoding: there must be sufficient attention (A) on the new material; learners must generate (G) their own connections to knowledge that they already have; moderate levels of emotion (E) are necessary; and coming back to the information regularly—spacing (S)—works wonders" (Davis et al. 2014).

In general, the OK-LCD model incorporates the AGES principles by:

- Using multiple learning assets creates more opportunities for attention and spacing.
- Ensuring learning is available across social, formal, and immediate contexts (or learning touchpoints) creates more occasions for generation and emotion.
- Encouraging crowdsourcing and learners' contributions to their own learning drives generation.

Figure 2-5. AGES Learning Theory

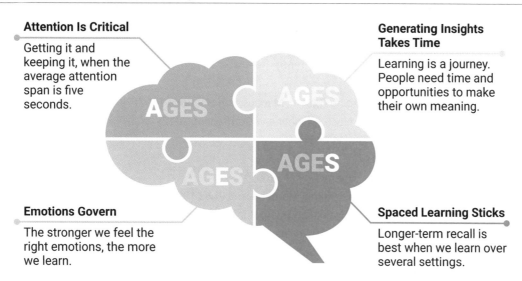

Attention Is Critical

Getting it and keeping it, when the average attention span is five seconds.

Generating Insights Takes Time

Learning is a journey. People need time and opportunities to make their own meaning.

Emotions Govern

The stronger we feel the right emotions, the more we learn.

Spaced Learning Sticks

Longer-term recall is best when we learn over several settings.

Does OK-LCD Replace My Other ID Models?

"No single ID model is well matched to the many and varied design and development environments in which ID personnel work. Hence ID professionals should be competent in applying and possibly adapting a variety of models to meet the requirements of specific situations." —Gustafson and Branch (2002)

Does the OK-LCD model replace all the other ID models? The short answer is no!

There are many great ID models that guide L&D in how to create effective learning from start to finish. Consider models such as ADDIE or SAM, or even Agile methods. However, we discovered that L&D's current ID models are all focused on designing a single learning asset. These ID models usually center on planned learning. The word *instructional* itself most often refers to planned learning. These models are designed to help you create learning that has a beginning and an end—even the iterative models. Some models will guide creation of a curriculum or a set of classes or courses, and we view this as great for designing one big learning asset.

But modern learning is about learning every day! Which is where OK-LCD comes in.

In contrast with existing ID models, the OK-LCD model operates in a context that is compatible with continuous, daily learning. As you'll see in chapter 3, on the Change Action, the OK-LCD model provides an umbrella objective for the entire set of learning assets within a learning cluster. The OK-LCD model is for inclusion of unplanned learning as well as planned learning. With the model, you are empowered to take on in-the-moment learning and move away from the notion that you can contribute only to top-down, controlled learning environments.

Some Supporting Learning Models and Theories

Perhaps you already know about these. If so, can you spot their influence on the OK-LCD model? Not familiar with this list? We invite you to learn more on your own.

- Adult Learning Principles (Knowles 1968)
- AGES (Davachi et al. 2010)
- Evaluation to Improve Learning (Bloom, Madaus, and Hastings 1981)
- Five Moments of Learning Need (Mosher and Gottfredson 2012)
- Conditions of Learning (Gagné 1965)
- Goal Analysis (Mager 1972)
- Individualized Instruction Theory (Keller 1960)
- Instructional Design Process (Kemp, Morrison, and Ross 1994)
- Kirkpatrick's Four Levels of Evaluation (Kirkpatrick and Kirkpatrick 2016)
- Situated Cognition Theory (Brown, Collins, and Duguid 1989)
- Sociocultural Learning Theory (Vygotsky 1915)
- Transactional Distance Theory (Moore 1997)

Having said that, both traditional ID models and emerging models work in harmony with the OK-LCD model (Figure 2-6). Here are a few examples of how we continue to leverage—not abandon—our time-honored expertise, and make use of the latest thinking from other thought leaders:

- **Bloom's Taxonomy.** Learning objective expertise plays a big role in successfully creating strategic performance objectives as well as standard terminal and enabling objectives.
- **Design Thinking.** Also known as human-centered frameworks, design thinking can be an alternative or additional way to gather data on your learners and deliver the Learn Action. (See chapter 4 for an example from Visa, where design thinking married with the OK-LCD model produced incredible results.)
- **ADDIE, SAM, and Agile.** These models primarily help design a single learning asset and therefore are used *after* the OK-LCD model has been applied. Once you have intentionally selected learning assets for your learning cluster, then it's time to apply theses traditional models as you design each learning asset. And you'll discover that the work done in the OK-LCD Actions feeds directly into these other models. This makes the single-asset design work go much quicker.
- **Kirkpatrick's Four Levels of Evaluation and other ROI methods.** These models help us measure the impact of learning and can be used to support the Track Transformation of Everyone's Results Action (see chapter 7). However, to get the desired results, these models must be addressed during the Change and Surround Actions. During the Change Action, use these models to help define initial business goals and learning objectives in a way that can be measured. During the Surround Action, make sure you've designed it in ways to measure the levels of impact for the wider variety of learning assets that will be used.

Figure 2-6. Harmony Between OK-LCD and Other ID Models

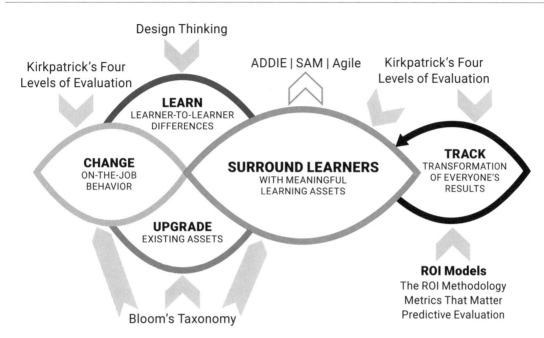

Solid blue arrows represent models that can serve as inputs to the OK-LCD Actions; the white arrow represents where the OK-LCD model provides an output for other models.

As our world gets more complex, our approaches must be able to navigate and work with the complexity, not ignore it. We believe the OK-LCD model, married with traditional approaches, will get us to our goal for impactful modern learning.

What's the OK-LCD Difference?

Recall the infographic of the evolution of L&D from chapter 1. It is a reminder that L&D has successfully served our businesses for a long time. And in a world where learning is needed every day, the role of L&D in the business is more important than ever. But our toolkit has become outdated. The OK-LCD model is a new tool to help us deliver modern learning (Figure 2-7).

Whether we are in a high-tech or low-tech industry, wherever there is a fast-paced and changing environment, businesses need L&D's expertise. They need our expertise on how to:

- Help learners learn—with teams and on their own.
- Sequence learning chunks to build learners' workplace capability.
- Engage both employees and leaders in learning—for the present and future.
- Match new learning technologies with true learner needs.
- Connect people with the best resources to enable purposeful learning.
- Strategically measure performance to ensure we all keep learning what's needed.

Figure 2-7. OK-LCD Model Shifts for the Training Industry

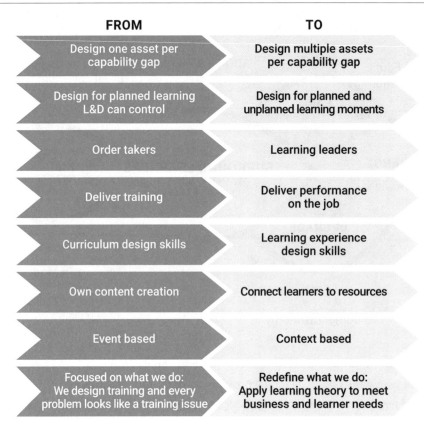

FROM	TO
Design one asset per capability gap	Design multiple assets per capability gap
Design for planned learning L&D can control	Design for planned and unplanned learning moments
Order takers	Learning leaders
Deliver training	Deliver performance on the job
Curriculum design skills	Learning experience design skills
Own content creation	Connect learners to resources
Event based	Context based
Focused on what we do: We design training and every problem looks like a training issue	Redefine what we do: Apply learning theory to meet business and learner needs

As you read the In Practice section here, you'll see how the infusion of the OK-LCD modern learning approach and philosophy have had a big impact in one high-tech company.

In Practice

Bluescape, a software-as-a-service company, sent its L&D team to our two-day workshop, where they became deeply grounded in the OK-LCD model and walked away with a learning cluster for one of their top priorities. Loc Nguyen, the L&D leader for Bluescape, said, "Before we shared the LCD approach with our team, many of us viewed training from a transactional perspective. We've been accustomed to the idea that customers pay for services, we show up to deliver content, and we leave with the hope that they've consumed enough to adopt our technology. For the most part, we've also been dependent on in-person sessions to effectively get the point across, which is obviously not scalable. It's certainly not a viable strategy if you're planning for thousands of customers. Everybody was in agreement with that."

However, Loc and his L&D teammates didn't have another way to think about training until they learned about the LCD model. Throughout the workshop, they diligently redesigned one of their existing learning initiatives by following the five Actions of the OK-LCD model. When they returned to work, they presented their learning cluster at a department-level meeting for the sales function.

"One of the turning points was when we revealed our new goal of building the cluster. We wanted to accommodate the various scenarios end users encounter within the Bluescape ecosystem, and we wanted to deliver the content they need during those learning moments. And that's when people were like, 'Wow, that's a good idea.'"

The L&D team built a full learning cluster, considering the on-the-job behavior change they wanted to see, the personas of the learners who would be taking the training, and the value of the existing assets. The results?

Loc reported: "As a result of all the work we did, even the most critical folks at Bluescape were personally on board with the methodology. More so, we now have funding for two more training specialists and possibly two more after that. It's amazing how just that fundamental shift has led to a new building phase with Bluescape."

Final Notes

Imagine if your L&D team got the same reaction from your organization to new initiatives as Bluescape got. How would you personally feel? Pretty good! And how would this change the organization's perception of L&D? Can you imagine how much more effective learning experiences would be? Or how much more efficient your team would be if enrolling support was that much easier?

We've seen firsthand the results that organizations get when applying the model (Figure 2-8). Together, with our consultant team, we have worked on complex learning challenges and delivered modern learning experiences that get results. Now, we encourage you to adopt the philosophy exemplified by the OK-LCD principles. And act! Follow the five Actions. Use the associated Tools to guide you. Create and deploy your own learning clusters and take note of the response from your

Figure 2-8. The OK-LCD Model Is . . .

business success-oriented

focused on changing on-the-job behavior

strategic and impactful

The Owens-Kadakia Learning Cluster Design model is . . .

learner-centric

balanced for speed and rigor

technology-infused

context-centered

L&D team, your business leaders, and most important, your learners. If you need help, reach out! From peer support to the latest research to support from the experts, you'll find that you, too, are surrounded by learning assets to create a new kind of L&D ready for the digital age.

In the next five chapters, you will read about the five Actions and Tools that make up the OK-LCD model. As you read, consider how you might achieve similar results as Loc Nguyen and Bluescape.

Reflect

Based on your reading so far, consider the following questions:
◊ What benefits can you envision for you and your L&D team when applying the OK-LCD model?
◊ When you compare the OK-LCD model with other ID models that you use, what is unique and different? What is similar and compatible?

Apply

◊ Take a moment to look at LearningClusterDesign.com. Find a phrase, story, or idea that inspires you to start the modern learning journey.
◊ Now, consider what you've seen so far and take a moment to create a mini-vision for yourself. What hopes do you have for your work? What is a goal you'd like to achieve?

3

Owning the Workplace, Not Just the Classroom

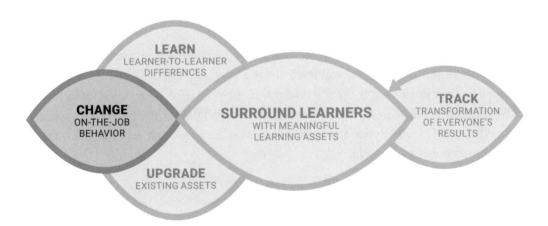

L&D evolves for the digital age when we take responsibility for improving performance on the job, rather than committing to only delivering the "by the end of this class" type of learning objectives. The OK-LCD model focuses on even higher-order objectives, the strategic performance objectives (SPOs). These SPOs state the connection between the capability gap and the desired changes to on-the-job behaviors and business measures. This new focus unlocks the possibility of creating multiple learning assets (that is, not just one training program per skill set) to provide learners with content they need, when, where, and how they need it. L&D continues to apply its core instructional design strengths, delivering rigorously designed programs based on strong learning objectives, but now in the form of learning clusters aimed at closing skills gaps and growing capability. As such, L&D is recognized as a driver of TD strategies and continues to move away from acting as order takers for delivering training programs.

The Change On-the-Job Behavior Action in the OK-LCD model is about setting a new goal for any L&D project. The moment you determine your goal is the moment you begin to shape the path to the solution and its related results (Figure 3-1).

CHANGE
ON-THE-JOB
BEHAVIOR

Figure 3-1. Our Goals Shape Our Solutions and Results

Goal: Create a Training Program	New Goal: Change On-the-Job Behavior
Results We Get:	Results We Desire:
☑ Attendance	💡 Epiphany
☑ Mastery in Controlled Environments	💡 Lightning or Aha Moments
☑ Passing Tests	💡 Behavior Change
☑ Regurgitation	💡 Perspective Change
☑ One-and-Done Training Events	💡 Higher Levels of Performance

The new goal is to change on-the-job behavior, as opposed to changing behavior by the end of a class or course. In this chapter, you will learn about a new goal for L&D, the impact of this new goal, and how you can implement it. As you read this chapter, imagine what it will mean for you and your L&D team to take this Action—to change on-the job behavior. Can you take on this higher-order responsibility? How will it affect your approach to designing learning? First, let's start with a story that takes place so often in our L&D world.

A Common L&D Story

Cast of Characters:

CEO
Doug

CFO
Marc

CHRO
Chris

CLO
Marissa

The Scene: Often, L&D conversations happen when L&D is not in the room! This is exactly the case as the chief human resources officer and the chief financial officer discuss the L&D budget and the justification for further investment.

"So, the bottom line is that Marissa is predicting the L&D budget projections will be up 8 percent versus last year to cover the costs of the LMS upgrade," Chris said to Marc. "With the dramatic increase in new hires, this LMS upgrade is crucial to ensuring that they all get trained up to do their jobs."

"Well, Chris, you know better than anyone how many people we are hiring, even if many of the new hires are simply replacing employees who left us," Marc replied with a shrug. "If you could give me some numbers to show that the investment would pay off, it would make it a whole lot easier to sell at next week's leadership meeting. . . . But never mind. You and I have discussed training ROI ad infinitum with no good resolution in sight."

"What I can tell you," Chris retorted, recalling her last conversation with Marissa, "is that the exit interviews for those regretted losses show that more than 60 percent of people who left said that they wanted more training and development opportunities. As soon as we get the LMS upgrade operational for new hires, Marissa says she's ready to shift the focus to using the LMS to get the right training to our other employees. We've got the courses for them to take, but they just aren't taking them. The LMS will help them and their managers see what is available for them to take. We're even considering creating some required training paths. This can help us ensure that employees are getting the training they need, despite their bosses who turn down training requests because of critical timing on a project. But, as you and I both know, there is always critical timing. Somewhere along the way, these employees need to be trained so they can do the job better, and faster."

"Yeah, the old 'stop chopping to sharpen the ax' story. I agree. I wish you luck with that one, Chris." Marc said. "OK. I'll go to the mat on this one for you. But what about next year? Are you planning to come to me with a request for a new e-learning platform, or maybe for virtual reality equipment? I was reading about that in an *HBR* article."

"Well, we *do* have to continue to modernize," Chris said with a smile. "VR equipment! Hmmm. I like that idea. I'll talk with Marissa's team about it."

"Just be careful, Chris." Marc said, returning the smile. "If you keep adding all that tech stuff, IT just might be tempted to try to take over and run your department!"

"You're a funny guy, Marc. But I'd like to see the IT department try to create the manager training that Doug has been asking for. Heck, the IT department can't even create the training for the new CRM program they are rolling out for the sales force—the L&D team is bailing them out on that debacle. So, I'm hoping to keep my job for the moment. Anyway . . . gotta run. Thanks for your help on the budget."

As Chris walked away, she reluctantly admitted to herself that the IT department might be able to create their own training; after all, it's so basic. But why would they bother if they could justify having L&D do it for them? L&D needs to be seen as strategic experts, not low-skilled outsourcers. Chris asked herself the question she's posed a million times: How does she support the L&D team to get there?

The Issues: How can the OK-LCD model make a difference for Chris, Marc, and their company? As you explore this chapter, form your own opinion on how to address these main issues:

- How do we justify training expenditures?
- How can we improve employee use of our training?
- How can we be more systematic about modernizing L&D?
- How can L&D enhance its reputation as learning experts who help deliver for the business?

The Action Explained

This Action is about modifying L&D's goals to increase our relevance and impact today. Historically, we in L&D have been strong on our use of goals and objectives. But with all the shifts in our world, let's consider how our current goals are limiting us, what new goals can rachet up our value to the business and our learners, and how we can use our new goals, coupled with multiple learning assets, to support performance improvement.

The Limitations of L&D Goals

Typically, we have defined our goals and our own success within the limitations of what can be accomplished in the classroom or by the end of a course. Why? Because this is what we feel we can control. It's how the business measures our value. The class or course is the product that stakeholders ask us to deliver. We want to deliver on our promises, and we believe that the only thing we can safely guarantee is the performance achieved at the end of a training course. But, this definition of L&D's goal dramatically limits our impact on the business.

Inherent in our old goals is that L&D would deliver one training course, and that's what learners would use. More than ever today, this fundamental assumption is just plain wrong. Learners use a variety of learning assets, whether L&D controls them or not. As you will soon see, L&D must now deliver multiple learning assets with a specific goal in mind (Figure 3-2).

Figure 3-2. A Single-Asset Solution Limits L&D's Impact

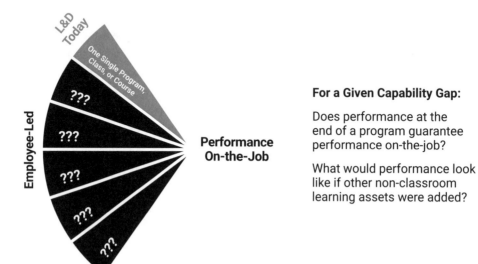

For a Given Capability Gap:

Does performance at the end of a program guarantee performance on-the-job?

What would performance look like if other non-classroom learning assets were added?

L&D professionals have long felt the need to have goals that go beyond the classroom. One way we have tried to go beyond the classroom and increase L&D's business relevance is by adding a return on investment (ROI) measure to our scorecard. Yet, despite the perceived importance of ROI, one McKinsey study found that only 8 percent of organizations track training ROI (Cermak and McGurk 2010). As Lidia Staron (2018) has noted, measuring ROI can be difficult because "measurements can be subjective. There's no single approach to measuring the ROI of employee training." We think it's time for a better goal.

A Better Goal: The Strategic Performance Objective

In this first Action in the OK-LCD model, Change On-the-Job Behavior, we create a higher-order goal in the form of a strategic performance objective (SPO).

What makes the strategic performance objective a higher order is two things. First, the SPO describes the linkage between the desired workplace behavior (not end-of-class behavior) and the benefits of this behavior for the business, in terms that the business cares about. In other words, it's about the connection between the business *strategy* and the employee *performance*. Second, the SPO is the overarching objective for a learning cluster. A learning cluster is the new product, composed of more than one learning asset, for L&D to enable us to achieve our new goals.

Our starting point is to identify the desired business impact, and then discern which on-the-job behavior changes are needed to deliver that business impact. This behavior change, once identified, becomes the target for all the learning assets in the learning cluster (Figure 3-3).

Figure 3-3. Writing the Strategic Performance Objective: A Reverse Engineering Approach

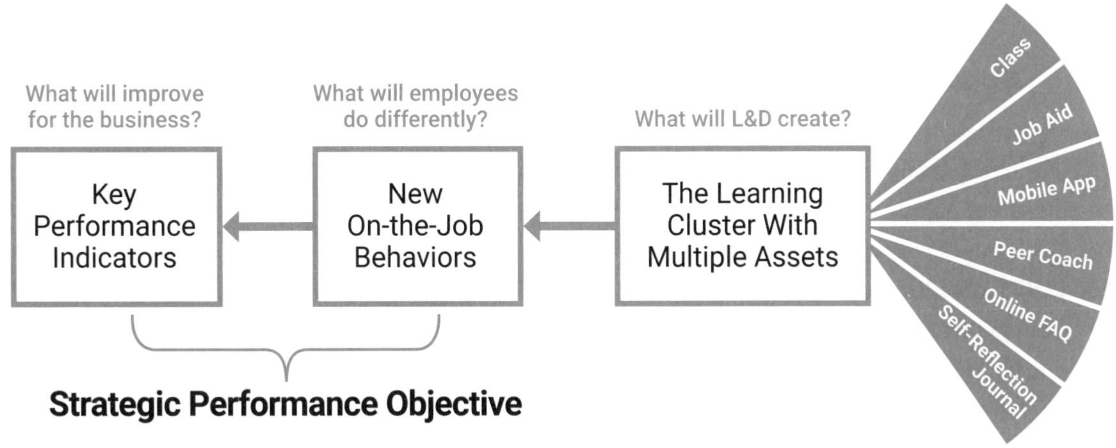

This new goal allows L&D to transcend the limitations of the class or course objectives of the past. It's more than shifting our focus outside of the classroom; it's about elevating our focus to include classroom and additional learning assets to empower learning by matching the most likely moments and ways people will need to learn.

Achieving the Goal With Multiple Learning Assets

Traditional instructional design is a form of reverse engineering that starts with learning objectives and adds the content that learners need so that they can achieve those objectives. The OK-LCD model takes it a notch higher (Figure 3-4).

Figure 3-4. The Strategic Performance Objective: A Higher-Order Goal, Shown in Two Ways

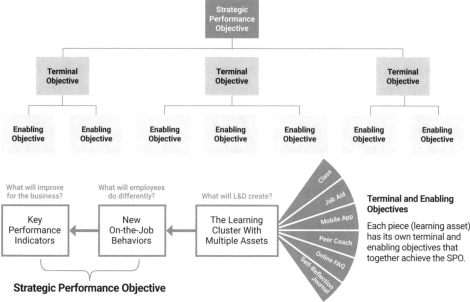

Our new learning goal hierarchy shows the strategic performance objective at the top, followed by a set of terminal objectives and enabling objectives. The lower levels are prerequisites for the higher levels.

With this new goal, L&D has a new focus: to help learners change their on-the-job behavior. In the OK-LCD model, we do this through learning clusters made up of numerous learning assets that L&D will strategically select and rigorously design, each with terminal and enabling learning objectives. This learning cluster:

- may include traditional classes and courses used away from the workplace
- can be used at the moment of learning need in the workplace to close a specific performance gap
- will also include a wide diversity of additional learning assets (for example, job aids, posters, mobile apps, blogs, classes, e-learning, social networks, infographics, virtual reality simulations, and so forth).

Remember Mosher and Gottfredson's Five Moments of Learning Need introduced in chapter 2? L&D has always wanted to be present for our learners in these moments, and we have historically attempted this by providing a course and some job aids and resources that they can use after the course.

In fact, many L&D professionals are already creating multiple learning assets. Maybe it's a class, plus a job aid; or an e-learning option, plus a memory card of the model; or a blended learning program with both online work and classwork. But at the moment, L&D seems to simply collect these learning assets or create them only as a need arises. There isn't a system or strategy to add these multiple learning assets for every learning goal.

In today's high-tech world, we can do better. The goal is to have strong L&D learning assets available to the learners at their fingertips when and where they need to learn. With the help of the OK-LCD model, we can provide seamless learning driven by the learner in and out of the flow of work, thus becoming more relevant for our organizations. And, as you'll see in chapter 6, we can do this without lots of extra work for L&D. In fact, it can be easier than trying to insert everything into a single class or course.

The OK-LCD model provides a strategy. It all starts with this first Action and our new goal: changing on-the-job behavior. For now, we will focus on the strategic performance objective—the new umbrella objective for the on-the-job behavior change—which will drive the formation of the lower-tiered terminal and enabling objectives for their related learning assets.

> "Historically, we inherited customers after the sales process, and we accommodated their needs, without a true training methodology. We created lots of content ad hoc and were driven in multiple directions. When we started going through all the work Crystal and Lisa put together, we both started to realize that this model was what we'd been lacking all along.

> "Over the last four years, we've been creating different types of training content out of necessity, not necessarily working toward the overall goal of aggregating that content and surfacing it strategically. So we had a light bulb moment during the workshop—now we understand what the overarching goal is and that there definitely has been an overarching goal [that is, the SPO]."
> —Loc Nguyen, L&D Leader at Bluescape Software

Not Familiar With Learning Objectives?

Instructional designers start with the end objective in mind and design down, identifying which prerequisite learning is needed or missing for the learner; learners start with the lower-level materials and learn up. The key to writing good objectives is to describe the visible behavior, which is an indicator that learning has happened in the learner's brain. A poor objective describes the things that an instructor does (teach them *xyz*), or that happen invisibly inside a learner's head (learn or know *xyz*). Taxonomies are models that help instructional designers provide content in a logical sequence to build the learner's skills.

If you're not familiar, take a moment to review this fundamental of instructional design. Try an online search for "importance of instructional objectives," looking for the key terms "Bloom's taxonomy" and "SMART objectives." Searching for images of "Bloom's objectives" is a fast way to get the big picture.

The Action Implemented

To help you accomplish the Change Action, we provide a tool to both step you through the process and guide your thinking as you go. The tool for the Change Action is a visual aid with a series of templates in a text document. The primary task during the Change Action is to craft a strategic performance objective. Later, when you are working on the Surround Action (chapter 6), you will continue to use the Change Tool to organize all the terminal and enabling objectives for your learning asset in the learning cluster you've designed. A full set of instructions for how to use the Change Tool is in the appendix, and an example of its use is in chapter 8. You can also find this tool at LearningCluster-Design.com/Book-Bonus. For now, let's focus on using this tool to write the strategic performance objective (Figure 3-5).

Figure 3-5. The Tool for the Change On-The-Job Behavior Action

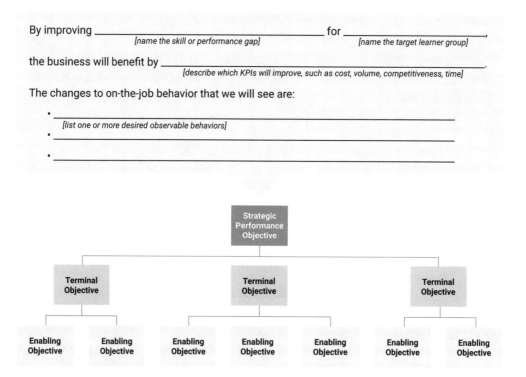

Parts of the Strategic Performance Objective

The strategic performance objective has several parts. Each part must be answered and tested with your stakeholders and customers:

- **Who** needs to change on-the-job performance (target learner).
- The name of the **skill or performance** being addressed.

- The business's **key performance indicator** (KPI) or other metrics that will improve as a result of using the learning cluster to close the performance gap.
- A description of **typical behaviors visible on the job** when the gap is closed. Usually three to five behaviors will be listed.

Getting the Data

Talking with leadership and key stakeholders is a crucial early step. The Change Action is not an exercise in trying to figure out what the learners will *know*; it's about capturing what stakeholders expect to *see* that is different when the learning cluster works as intended. Remember, these people will be focused on trying to get you to give them a training program, so you will have to use your best interviewing skills to ferret out what behavior change they expect to see in the workplace and what business measures will improve as a result of this learning cluster. The tool will help you verbalize this. Read through the real example in the In Practice section to see how to draw out behavior-change goals from stakeholders.

During your interviews, pay special attention to the following:

- For the who, be specific. Instead of "R&D people," a deeper dive might result in "R&D people doing chemical testing in a laboratory"; instead of "manufacturing employees," you might get "anyone who walks onto the manufacturing floor, including administrators and visitors."
- Find a KPI that the business cares about and may already be tracking. The KPI may be the underlying reason for the request for more training.
- For typical behaviors that will be visible when performance improves, seek specifics or, at a minimum, several examples. We tend to start with this component because people seem to be able to describe this more easily than KPI. Then we'll work our way back to the other components of the strategic performance objective.

L&D Skills at Work

L&D has many valuable skills that are helpful when crafting a strategic performance objective and for designing a learning cluster. Here are a few L&D skills useful for the Change Action:

- interviewing
- writing solid learning objectives
- project management
- needs analysis
- problem solving
- strategic thinking
- systems thinking.

Here's an example of a complete strategic performance objective (more examples are in Figure 3-6).

By getting marketers (who) up to speed quickly on the new CRM software (desired performance), the business will benefit by a two-point gain in positive customer metrics (KPI). In the workplace:

- We will see marketers accessing the old database less frequently after five days beyond the go-live date (behavior).
- Additionally, each team will agree to sign off on archiving the old system within one month of the go-live date, thus reducing the cost of running two systems simultaneously (extra behaviors, KPIs, and benefits).

Did you notice that we applied the template flexibly? The SPO template is a guide, not a required format. Use the thinking behind the template to guide your work.

Figure 3-6. Examples of Each Part of the Strategic Performance Objective

Target Learner	Capability Gap	KPI	On-the-Job Behaviors
Project team members	Time-to-market capability	Reduce project completion time by 5% vs. historical 5-year average to match Tier 1 competition.	• The Stage Gate process is used for every project to ensure project teams are aligned on goals and able to provide management with the necessary information to quickly make go or no-go decisions.
Workers and their supervisors	Safety compliance	Reduce lost-time accidents to a level 20% lower than industry norms.	• Employees quote safety rules and regs to one another while planning and performing their work, thereby encouraging one another to "do it safely." • The "do it safely" motto is heard regularly on the manufacturing floor.
Managers of others	Manager relationship-building skills	Undesirable turnover is below industry averages.	• Calendar entry analysis (by IT) reveals more one-on-one meetings between managers and their employees. • Managers will be heard using the language of the personality trait and strengths assessment to describe employees or job openings. • Managers can be seen making the rounds among employees, and are heard offering assistance, support, and compliments.
Lab workers	Regulatory compliance	50% fewer minor violations with no significant outages, thereby reducing effort hours spent on after-audit issues.	• They regularly tour labs doing SOP inspections for their assigned SOP. • They talk with others about SOP improvements. • They submit regular SOP updates as improvements are identified. • Everyone consults SOPs and FDA regulations handbook. • All use check sheets required for every task.

In Practice

At a Fortune 100 company, a client requested that last year's mandatory training on executive compensation be delivered again to all the top managers. The director of compensation explained it to the new L&D manager like this:

"We created this half-day training course to explain how the new compensation program is designed to encourage managers to make decisions that will be balanced between what is good for their own organization and for the company as a whole. These folks just didn't listen the first time. They didn't understand it, or they didn't remember the training. We have to run this training course again."

When asked what the executives needed to do differently, the director went into a litany of decision-making processes and lengthy descriptions of how the compensation system managed the balance of "for me" and "for all of us" decisions. After some time, the L&D leader asked, "So if I design a new training course for you, how will you know it works? What will be different?" The director responded with passion, "My phone will quit ringing off the hook with calls from the executives asking me to explain it again!"

It was this one insight—that the executives need to quit calling the director for help on making balanced decisions—that led to the formation of an entirely different set of learning assets. The new class was just one hour and helped executives apply a new set of learning assets. The assets enabled them to independently learn and get answers at the point in time when they were considering a decision that could affect both their compensation and the company's success.

A few months after the new learning assets were deployed, the director called the L&D manager to say thanks. "My phone has stopped ringing, and I'm now able to get to my other tasks. It worked!"

The Action's Impact

For the Change Action, we covered the what and the how. Now, let's shift gears and consider the impact of this Change Action on you, the L&D practitioner. But first, let's start with a story, one that might happen in your world when you begin to apply the OK-LCD model. Remember the common story at the beginning of the chapter? Let's look at how the L&D team begins to transform by using the OK-LCD model.

An OK-LCD Story

Cast of Characters:

CEO
Doug

CMO
Raj

CLO
Marissa

The Scene: Doug and Raj both arrived a bit early for a meeting and do a bit of catching up before it starts.

"Hi Doug. How's it going?" asked Raj as he took his seat at the conference room table.

"Good," Doug replied. "Hey, recall our conversation about training last week? Well, Marissa and I met about the training for our people managers. She was asking some different questions this time," Doug said with a hint of pleasant surprise.

"Same here," Raj said. "Marissa and I met about the training on the new CRM software upgrade. She asked me, 'How will you know if the training was a success?' I told her that it's her job to tell me if the training is successful or not! But she was hunting for different information. She wanted to know what I would see in people that would be different in the workforce and in the workplace if the training took. She said she was formulating a 'strategic performance objective.'"

Doug frowned. "Interesting. She said similar things to me when she and I met about the manager training I'd requested. My immediate response to her 'what would be different' question was that employees would stay on the job and quit leaving unexpectedly! She was OK with that answer and requested a list of managers to talk to for more insights. And she asked for access to exit interview data. She said she'd figure out some root causes related to managers' impact on employee turnover, then she'd create the material and track which organizations and managers are using it. She said she needed a business resource to help determine if there's a correlation between using the training class and the strategic performance objective about undesirable turnover."

Raj interjected: "But she didn't call it 'training classes' when we talked. She was talking about something called, what was it . . .?"

"Learning clusters?"

"Yeah, that's it," Raj said. "Learning clusters and learning assets. She said she's on a path to modernize our training, and that's the new modern lingo for her deliverables. She said that if I want modern training, I have to let her put different learning assets out in the workplace where our employees can get to them easily. She asked for server space, permissions to write to our Share-Point site, a regular feature article on our marketing homepage, and a few other things. As usual, she asked for a few experts who can help deliver the training class or webinar, but said they'd likely spend just half the time that they usually spend on these types of training courses. She said that with the modern learning approach of learning clusters, the class time would likely be shorter. That was music to my ears."

"Shorter, huh? That's unexpected," Doug said. "I also didn't expect her to turn down my offer to make the manager training mandatory. She said that some people prefer to learn using different training stuff . . . I mean learning assets. She pushed me to think about what difference we wanted for the business. Based on that, she said that what she really needs is for the leadership to make it well known that we are reviewing managers' turnover rates on a quarterly basis and will be holding managers accountable for poor rates. Then she'd do the rest."

Doug continued with a smile, "What I liked best about her new strategy is that she says she can get improved performance without a big budget increase to implement the modernization program. She just needs some patience and support with the new thinking. I think I'm going to like this modernization program—it sounds a lot more connected to what we are really trying to achieve."

The OK-LCD Difference: Now, L&D connects clearly with the business, rather than the business having to fill in the blanks itself. L&D has the opportunity to deliver on the business goal, as guided by its instructional design expertise, rather than being limited to the training product the business asks for in the moment.

The impact of the Change Action is significant and can differ based on your own unique context. In the OK-LCD Story sidebar, the leadership noticed the change as L&D began using the model. But to get to this place, L&D practitioners need to reconsider some deeply ingrained perspectives. This includes our perspective on our purpose, our area of responsibility, our language, and our control over learning materials.

L&D people typically:
- Care about helping others.
- Like continuous and varied learning.
- Demonstrate strong analytical skills.
- Apply rigor and structured thinking.
- Embrace efficiency and order.
- Communicate well.
- Have an eye for detail.
- Are creative.
- Are experts on how people learn.

None of this changes; but how we apply our characteristics and skills will change, as L&D continues to evolve. In the past, the L&D organizational purpose was to "create training." L&D people had to be subject matter experts (SMEs). Now, with the preponderance of information, and the speed of change in nearly every field of study, being the all-knowing SME is no longer feasible or desirable.

Our new purpose is to empower on-the-job performance. It is to be brave enough to guarantee that our learning clusters will deliver the strategic performance objective, complete with new behaviors seen in the workplace. We accomplish this by surrounding people with learning assets to help them learn when, where, and how they need to learn. As we will explore further in the Surround Action in chapter 6, we can accomplish this in new ways, such as:

- curating information to provide effective reminders and spaced learning
- providing infrastructure for experts to communicate newfound knowledge
- providing pathways to help learners efficiently get to the right content
- connecting people to resources (mentors, experts, blogs, books) for learning
- teaching people how to learn and remember (applying neuroscience findings)
- crowdsourcing content to help all benefit from the wisdom of the crowd.

These are new ways of thinking about our deliverables. Yet, with L&D's skills—such as knowing what has to be learned in what preferred order, and how to chunk things—we can expand our deliverables beyond standard training materials to an entirely new set of learning assets.

Expand to a Future Mindset Beyond the Class

The future mindset for L&D is about taking responsibility for what happens beyond the class. This can be tough because, currently, L&D doesn't believe they have any control outside the classroom or that our job includes developing learning assets outside of one or two top-down, controlled programs. Plus, it feels like the number of variables expands uncontrollably when we look into the workplace.

Today's scorecards touch on only formal, not informal, learning methods. Without measures, we may feel we cannot prove our worth—even to ourselves! Look to the Upgrade, Surround, and Track Actions, where you'll discover ways to manage these concerns.

The Change Action is about L&D taking responsibility for what happens in the workplace, where high-speed learning is needed. This is not about eliminating classes and courses—these are still very much needed!

As we share the OK-LCD approach, we've noted that too many L&D professionals are so divorced from the business that they cannot make any link between their training and the business's success. This has to change! L&D needs to be asking the leadership, "If learners succeed in the training, what will be different in the workplace? And why do you think that difference will be a benefit to the organization?"

Upgrade Your Language

The harsh truth for L&D is that our goal is not to train content; our goal is to drive business success by enabling learning that changes some defined on-the-job behavior. Yet when we talk with L&D professionals about what they do, it's all about delivering training. Upgrade your language! Use the modern L&D language of *strategic performance objective* and *learning clusters*. This is one of the early steps L&D can take to gain authority for and take responsibility for improving performance outside of formal training. L&D gains immediate business attention simply by talking about delivering a *strategy* instead of a *program*. We get even more attention when talking about how we want to link learner performance to both the workplace actions and to desired business outcomes. Users of the OK-LCD model have been surprised how this one step can help shift people's thinking, both inside and outside L&D, from a focus on "our own L&D turf"—the controlled, formal training—to the broader workplace where performance occurs.

Cede Control for the Greater Good

Because content has been democratized and readily available to anyone with a connection to the Internet, L&D cannot control what is learned. Instead, we need to shift our focus from only *what* they learn, to include *that* they learn.

If the L&D industry hangs on to our former role of being the owners and deliverers of content, we will become as quaint as a candle factory during the golden age of electricity. Instead, let's use our L&D skills to aid others in sharing their content, crowdsourcing quality of content, learning how to learn, and finding high-quality content quickly when the need arises (Figure 3-7).

Figure 3-7. Summary of Mindset Changes Driven by the OK-LCD Model

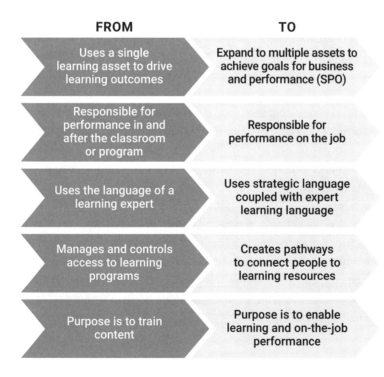

In Practice

Crystal encountered a large Fortune 500 company undergoing a huge culture change in its manufacturing organization—from a single-skilled to a multiskilled technician team. Like many organizations, it had all the manuals and guides prepared, but hadn't thought much about training implementation and change management.

The company's external management consultant was prepared to bring technicians into the classroom and take them through 600-slide PowerPoint decks with SME lecturers. Instead, the company asked for Crystal's help, and she began introducing and applying the OK-LCD model to the challenge. The Change Action immediately provided a key insight. The initial learning objective was "to teach the technician team 20 new work processes." So far, the internal team had been focused on *what* the employees needed to know, but very little on what the employees were expected to *do* with the information—let alone what else would need to *change* as a part of the cultural shift. In addition, there were three audiences for the content, not just one. The team had been applying the same learning objectives to three separate audiences.

Through conversations with manufacturing and supply chain leaders in charge of the culture change, Crystal was able to draw out the true business need and communicated it as this strategic performance objective:

> *By enabling the technician team and its supporting leadership in the new multiskilled teamwork processes, the business will benefit by being ready to start meeting phase one reliability, safety, and employee engagement targets [as specified in the organization's detailed phase progression chart outlining key performance indicators]. The on-the-job behaviors we expect to change are for workers to:*
> - *articulate the difference between the old world and the new, specifically what the change in old work processes look like, how their behavior will shift, and how they are rewarded in the new culture*
> - *demonstrate new bonds with their brand-new team, and adherence to co-created norms for working together.*

Rather than memorizing the intricate, end-to-end details of each new work process, the strategic performance objective shifted the focus of the learning to simply being able to recognize what's different while highlighting the importance of the social learning that needed to take place to ensure a successful launch. You can imagine how this new target began to expand the team's mindset, from delivering 600 slides of content to providing different learning assets geared toward what was important for job performance.

Final Note

In this chapter, we introduced the first Action of the OK-LCD Model, Change On-the-Job Behavior. We discussed the crucial elements of the Change Action; the difference they make to building effective, modern L&D deliverables; and the tool that brings it to life. We describe how L&D needs to elevate our focus to a new objective—the strategic performance objective—that targets results beyond the end of a single learning asset. We shared how identifying the most important key performance indicators and on-the-job behaviors are at the heart of this Action. Lastly, we discussed the mindset shifts that will support you on your journey as you begin the Change Action. The mind shifts can be rather dramatic and include rethinking our purpose, our language, and what we control.

We believe that in the future, L&D can better deliver on employee development goals by starting with a strong foundation of the higher-level strategic performance objectives. To support you in accomplishing this, consider using some of the learning assets listed here to supplement or reinforce what you have gained from this chapter:

- The Change Tool. We've included the most recent version for you in the appendix. For future evolutions or for support writing a SPO for your next initiative, head to LearningClusterDesign.com/Book-Bonus.
- The learning cluster on how to use the OK-LCD model, located in chapter 9. We designed this to help you grow your capability to use the model in your workplace. Again, see the website for updates.
- Chapter 8, which provides a full example of the OK-LCD model in practice.
- The chapters on the other Actions in the OK-LCD model, so that you can see how each Action supports the others.

Reflect

◊ How might the OK-LCD language affect how leadership views L&D? Which language changes do you think are most impactful or important?

◊ What pushback do you foresee as you make the transition to the OK-LCD model? How will you deal with this pushback from leaders and key stakeholders?

◊ Consider the issues our common story characters had at the beginning of the chapter. Ask how could the OK-LCD model make a difference with the following issues:
- justifying training expenditures
- improving employee use of our training
- systematically modernizing L&D
- enhancing L&D's reputation as learning experts who help deliver the business.

Apply

◊ Consider a recent learning initiative you worked on. If you consider the terminal objectives for that initiative, what would a higher-level strategic performance objective look like?

- What KPIs would you include?
- What on-the-job behaviors do you think your stakeholders and customers are interested in changing?
- What would your process look like for identifying the data and validating the strategic performance objective statement?

◊ Take a look at the tool in the appendix or head to LearningClusterDesign.com/Book-Bonus. Fill out each section to gain deeper practice in the Change On-the-Job Behavior Action.

4

Creating Experiences As Unique As Your Learners

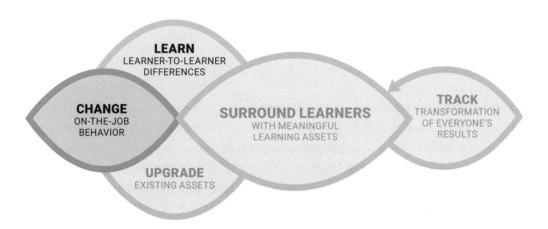

Instead of delivering a one-size-fits-all approach, modern L&D considers deeply who the learners are, and what learning assets might accelerate their skill development. In the Learn Action, build on the Change Action by using a data-driven approach to segment the target learner group into several meaningful learner personas. Then identify the personas whose behavior change will have the greatest effect on the desired business results. Persona definitions go beyond demographics and job type, to explore the learners' contexts of when, where, and how each persona will most likely need the learning. Rather than losing energy learning in ways that don't fit their situation, learners are more engaged when L&D shows that we understand and have created assets based on learner-to-learner differences.

In the industrial age, there were often only one or two paths available to get to a desired outcome. People had to adapt to these paths, even if it didn't work as well for their needs. L&D had the luxury of using and honing the same path over and over again, creating great efficiencies—whether that was a classroom lesson, a book, or a program. Within that path, we in L&D have always considered our variety of learners and tailored the design to create strong learning experiences. We have an expertise for analyzing and serving our target audience.

LEARN
LEARNER-TO-LEARNER
DIFFERENCES

However, in the digital age, technology has empowered learners to have countless paths to a desired outcome. And modern learners will use these paths to meet their learning needs—even though the paths to learning are not always the best paths to get the results they and the business are looking for. For any topic that learners want to explore, through today's technology, they can:

- Find copious content—articles, videos, and much more.
- Search for people who are world experts.
- Contact experts, practitioners, or peer learners.
- Chat through blogs with experts and practitioners.
- Call a peer, manager, or friend for help or advice.
- Take courses.
- Get microcertifications.

All this is at their fingertips. So, if we in L&D don't use our expertise to create access to the best content and learner experiences, and make it available when, where, and how today's learners need it, then we cannot affect the productivity of employees in the business. Instead, employees will end up spending their limited time searching instead of learning. It's up to us to build the best, most efficient path for needed learning, even in our fast-paced, ever-changing environment.

In the Learn Learner-to-Learner Differences Action, you discover segments within your primary learner group and uncover the most likely moments of learning need for each. This information is crucial input as you design the best learning assets for these target learners in later Actions. In this chapter, you'll read about the common uses of personas and their place in our L&D toolbox, how to create learner personas for your own learning projects, and the positive impact personas can have on modern learning design.

A Common L&D Story

Cast of Characters

Employee
Jaik

Manager
Julia

CMO
Raj

The Scene: In a small meeting room, Julia is wrapping up a performance review meeting with Jaik.

"So, to summarize, Jaik, your performance is good," Julia said with a smile. "And you are on track for advancement when a position opens up. The only thing holding you back is your project management capability. Based on what our boss's boss said, Raj and the others in the C-suite are unhappy with project delivery times. They want everyone to go through training on this. I don't know what the L&D department will come up with, but I want you to get ahead of the curve. I'd like you to focus on improving your project management skills. And I'd like to be able to demonstrate to the promotion-approval team that you've improved in this area."

"How can I do that?" Jaik asked, his voice betraying a little emotion. He found performance reviews to be tough meetings, but he was more than willing to learn and develop his skills.

"I'm not sure, but let's try to map out a plan. Let's start with the L&D catalog," Julia said. "There's a PDF of course listings somewhere on the HR website." After a few minutes of searching, she told Jaik, "Here's a course for new project managers. You could sign up for that. I know you aren't a project manager per se, but you might as well get the best skill set to help lead your project team."

"Could I take an outside course instead?" Jaik asked.

"Sure. An outside course is likely better than anything we have in-house. That might put you ahead of some of the other candidates. Just be sure to send me your certificate of completion so I can add that to your file when promotion time comes around."

"OK, sure, but do you have any other ideas about how to build my project management skills? To be honest, I'm not too keen on taking training," Jaik admitted. "If I studied on my own at home, maybe read a few books?"

"Those are good ideas, Jaik. Look for materials from PMI. That's a global project management accreditation group. They should have something that's just right for you." Julia paused to think a moment. "If I knew some good PMs, I'd send you their names so you could contact them for some coaching, but no one comes to mind. I know you can do this, Jaik. You just have to get your projects delivered on time. I don't care what it takes. You are a smart guy. You'll figure it out."

"Yes ma'am!" He gave a smile and salute. "I'm on my way to do good stuff!" he declared; he grabbed his notes and waved as he headed out of the meeting room.

The Issues: How can the OK-LCD model's Learn Action make a difference for Julia and Jaik? As you dig into this chapter, form your own opinion on how to address these main issues:
- How can we provide a broader array of pathways to support the various ways learners want to learn?
- How might we build employee trust in the quality of in-house learning assets?
- How could we customize learning assets to more closely target individual learning needs?

The Action Explained

The Learn Action is about how you in L&D can more easily meet the needs of modern learners. A modern learner is someone who needs to learn fast in an ever-changing environment, and who will access a wide variety of resources to get answers. This is a broad definition of L&D's customer in today's work world. It includes Millennials and Gen Z, but it is not exclusive to relatively recent generations. It includes digital tools, but not exclusively. These learners want more than one-size-fits-all learning solutions.

You want to be the one who guides them to the "best for me" learning resources, be it a class, an e-learning course, a book, a mentoring program, a certification program, a webinar, virtual instructor-led training, or a blog. But given the diversity of resources out there, how do you figure out which ones the learners will appreciate and want to use?

In this section, we describe some differences between the OK-LCD approach and the typical L&D approach to analyzing a target audience; the value of the learner persona technique, which is part of the Learn Tool; and a few guidelines for persona creation.

Comparing Approaches: From Target Audience to Learner Personas

In a typical ADDIE process, understanding your target audience is part of the Analyze phase. For some projects, there is deep analysis of the target learner, complete with interviews, surveys, and even job shadowing. Other times, designers talk to a few SMEs and maybe some learners or stakeholders. It's common to get a description of the target learners from the project sponsor, or to base the description on L&D's previous experience with this group. The end product is a single, monolithic description of the target audience that will guide the design and development of the learning asset.

In contrast, the OK-LCD model devotes an entire Action to learner understanding. In the Learn Action, you will dig deeper to gather different data about the context for the learners and their moments of learning need. You'll analyze the data, looking for distinct differences, and develop multiple learner personas. You'll pinpoint which personas will have a proportionally larger impact on the desired business results if their behavior changes. The Learn Action is heavily influenced by the Change Action's strategic performance objective, as you segment the target learner group into the crucial learner personas.

A learner persona is a descriptive story that goes beyond demographics into behaviors, attitudes, and the day-to-day life of a subgroup of the target learner group—things that can and will affect your learning cluster design.

Here is a simple example that demonstrates the difference. You've been asked to develop a training program on a new safety strategy for a manufacturing organization. Your target learner group is the safety leaders across the company who need to apply this safety strategy where they work, at various manufacturing plants around the world. As you read these two scenarios, consider which one is most likely to deliver learning assets that the learners will say are "best for me":

- **Scenario One:** You design a class in which the safety leaders go through all the content related to the new safety strategy. The class includes role-play activities to help learners practice the new safety strategy, as well as to get ideas from one another about how to implement this new strategy. To ensure that learning transfers to the workplace, you provide a physical job aid as a takeaway for each participant.
- **Scenario Two:** You dig deeper into the safety leader population and discover that different types of manufacturing plants have different types of safety hazards. In addition, you become aware of significant cultural differences. You create a class with role play and social learning ideas, but to account for differences, you tag content sections based on which type of plant the participants are coming from. The trainer can choose which sections to include, based on the safety hazards that will be encountered by the learners in a particular class. This reduces class time by focusing only on the relevant hazards, rather than teaching everyone everything. Next, to address cultural differences, you create variations on role-play activities, and you coach the trainers on how to match these variations to the differing cultural needs of the class participants as they deliver the class around the world. You also begin to think about other learning assets outside the classroom, beyond the one job aid, that would be helpful to particular locations. See the summarized outcome (Figure 4-1).

Figure 4-1. Comparing Two Learner Scenarios

	Scenario One	Scenario Two
Approach	Target Audience: Safety Leaders	Target Learner Personas: Safety Leaders From Eastern vs. Western Cultures; Safety Leaders From Chemical vs. Mechanical vs. Power Plants
Learning Design Ideas	All leaders: • Role play. • Brainstorm ideas socially. • Get physical job aids to take with them.	Depending on the location or the trainer: • uses particular hazard content and ignores others • varies role plays for greater participation and learning • provides particular job aids and assets by location.

Which scenario do you think will make the most movement toward the business goal: the one target audience, or the handful of learner personas? Which scenario builds more loyalty and confidence in the quality of L&D's products?

The Value of Personas

The term *persona* comes from marketing. Marketers build personas to align with the mindset of their customers. Marketers are then better able to design products that will resonate across the diversity of their target customers. Persona use increases the likelihood that customers will purchase and enjoy the product. When using the product, the customers are able to fill a need or solve a problem they have. Doesn't this sound like things you need as well?

You need employees to choose your products, find your products helpful, and ultimately, use it to solve their capability or performance challenge. Typical demographic data, such as the size of the target learner group, tenure, function, or location, don't tell you enough about your learners to design learning assets that will be loyally used. Research shows that we in L&D could benefit from a deeper understanding of the mindset of our customers (Figure 4-2).

Figure 4-2. How Is L&D Doing at Meeting Learner Needs?

Source: Rich (2015) and Greany (2018).

Research from Elucidat shows that employees have only 1 percent of their time set aside for learning, and so learning must happen within the flow of the work (Greany 2018). Yet, L&D traditionally has considered a target audience only when they are in the classroom or taking a course. The Learn Action can help you better understand the *when* of learning, which may be very different for each learner persona. If we provide learners what they need when they need it, they will become loyal to our learning products and agree that the training we designed is "best for me"!

Some Guidelines for Persona Creation

To create and select these personas, look to the strategic performance objective for help. There could be countless ways to divide our target learner group. What we want is to focus on the learner personas that give us the most confidence that we will close the gap outlined in the strategic performance objective.

Once you understand the major differences within your target learner group, turn your findings into data you can use for learning cluster development by investigating and writing meaningful stories of the day-to-day life and the point of view for each learner persona. The most meaningful stories are those that inform us of factors that influence learning asset usage and learning transfer. What do they need to know? What does their flow of work look like, and how can they learn the best in that flow of work? When will they need the learning? Where will they be when they want or need to learn? These are just a sample of the kinds of questions this Action aims to explore.

Learner persona creation represents an art in balancing generality and specificity. You need enough information to be smart about selecting learning assets, but not so much information that you have an infinite number of personas. Your set of learner personas—typically only three to five—should be general enough that 80 to 90 percent of your target learner group could fit into them.

In Practice

In Crystal's work, she has come across a variety of clients where learner personas made a critical difference to the outcome of the initiative. For one manufacturing client, implementation of a new work process required a new role: an assessor. The assessor's job would be to determine—or assess—the progress their site was making toward implementing this new work process. The training was to be focused on upskilling these newly named assessors.

As she developed a strategic learning objective for the project, Crystal identified a business risk —a significant waste of time if the training did not address standardization of assessments across the company. If assessors delivered assessments, or "grades," that were different from site to site, the result was likely chaotic, with communication breakdowns and negative competition among sites. It's the equivalent of one high-school teacher giving an A for work that another teacher graded as a C. The company needed a uniform way for the assessors to do their job.

Crystal introduced the idea of learner personas and began doing interviews to determine who might pose a risk to standardized assessments. She worked off the initial hunch that location and pre-existing familiarity with the work process would be big factors. If they didn't know the work process well enough, they may not be able to judge it in a standard way. If they were in a different location, culture might be an issue with how assessment results were reported. With the client's help, she interviewed people at a diverse range of sites, in multiple regions.

The interviews confirmed her initial hunch, and further revealed that the size of manufacturing site was also an important factor. Site size influenced the length of time needed to conduct an assessment, and correlated with the assessment's complexity. The interviews also showed that some concerns the L&D team had about this global project were not as important, such as years of experience at the company. Based on the learner persona work, it was recommended that assessors at more complex sites have access to additional learning assets to help them at their point of need. The company valued the insights, and the learners from both small and large manufacturing sites benefited.

The Action Implemented

The Learn Tool walks you through five steps for creating a set of learner personas for your project. The end goal when using the Learn Tool is to create a short story for those personas that are critical to meeting the strategic performance objective (from the Change Action). These stories describe the key differences between the learners, differences that, when highlighted, may inspire use of different learning assets. An abbreviated form of the tool is shown in Figure 4-3. Here are the highlights of those steps.

Figure 4-3. Learn Learner-to-Learner Differences Tool (Abbreviated)

1. **Summarize** what you already know.

2. **Dig deeper** into learner differences. Identify needed information and how to get it.

3. **Analyze to create learner persona profiles.** The following categories are recommended:

   - Persona name
   - Key demographic differences
   - Key learning-need differences

   - Key life-at-work differences
   - Key performance gap difference
   - Moments of learning need

4. **Create the learner persona stories,** complete with name and avatar.

Persona 1: Lax Sam	Persona 2:
 Lax Sam is an individual contributor with a few years of experience. His biggest challenge to time management is that he's overbooked (including for training!) and that he doesn't use any systems to help understand the enormity of each task he commits to doing.	

5. **Use the persona** to guide learning asset selection and design. List asset ideas here.

Persona 1: _____	Persona 2: _____
• • •	• •

First, **summarize what you already know**. Whether it's from previous projects with this group, or provided by the project sponsor, this information creates a good start for the Learn Action. Especially important is the answer to the question, "Do you have an initial idea about who within the learner group is causing the most concern, or who would benefit the most from this performance improvement?" In the next step, you will either test your theory or get an answer to the question.

Second, **dig deeper**. Map out the work before you start digging. There are two types of maps. First, map out or outline what information you think you may need, and then map out a plan to efficiently get the data. The Learn Tool can provide additional ideas and support. Here is a short list of things to be sure to cover in your L&D learner analysis:

- Who needs this training the most? Who is preventing the organization from meeting your business goal? (Reminder: You may already have some ideas based on your Change Action work.)
- Typical response to training or learning: love it, hate it, already know it all, discomfort.
- Primary technology used on the job: go-tos for learning assets or performance support.
- Preferred learning go-tos: class, e-learning, video, self-assessments, experts.
- Life-at-work differences: level of discretionary time, network for learning, best time to learn.
- Likely moments of learning need: Is this new learning? More learning? Learning about changes? What's the learner context for applying and troubleshooting?

The third step is to **analyze the data you collected**. This is a very creative step. We encourage you to read the section of the Learn Tool in the appendix called "The Art of Knowledge Analysis for Creating Learner Personas." During this step, you identify the personas and give them a name and an avatar, or face, focusing on those personas that are likely to have a big impact on delivering the strategic performance objective.

The fourth step is to **create the persona story**—that is, to crystalize your communication about the learner persona by boiling it down to an illustrative story of who and what this persona is all about. Again, this step is part art, and L&D professionals, in our experience, can be very good at distilling the essence into something meaningful. It's worth testing your personas with key stakeholders. Did you characterize the groups well? Is there a missing piece of data that can provide more insight? By checking back with stakeholders, you also continue to build the confidence of others in the organization about your learning products and their quality.

The final step is to **identify what would meet the learner persona needs**. Use your persona work to get a head start on the Upgrade and Surround Actions. With the newly crystalized learner personas clearly in your head, list what types of learning assets might be most inviting to them so they want to choose these learning products off the virtual L&D grocery store shelf.

All this material can be nicely bundled up and used when it's time to do the detailed design and development of individual learning assets. In some companies, they've done enough learner personas to create a catalog of personas. However, the catalog approach comes with a caution: Personas must be considered based on their relationship to the strategic performance objective. Depending on the problem or goal, the nature of the persona groupings can change significantly. Use the lens of the SPO to guide you during this Learn Action.

In Practice

Sravani Tammiraju leads the onboarding process for the technology and operations employees at Visa. When redesigning the onboarding process, she combined the OK-LCD model with design thinking to create powerful results. Specifically, for the Learn Action, design thinking served as Sravani's primary process to gather information about her learners. Empathy interviewing techniques gave her ideas on what would resonate most directly with learners and stakeholders. But, as she realized, "What you get from the design thinking method is a lot of data points—and those data points are scattered everywhere. Learning cluster design really helped define what that experience would look like. It helped me make sure those data points were utilized in the most effective way."

Sravani's story is a great example of how to use other modern learning design processes as compatible partners with the OK-LCD model to deliver products that learners value. The learners' response was stellar, as you will see in the Visa in Practice sidebar in chapter 7, on the Track Action.

The Action's Impact

To get the benefits from the Learn Action, there are a few mindset shifts to make. First and foremost, you should be willing to reach learners at their moments of learning need, rather than prioritizing where and when L&D is available. Second, recognize that inside your learner group are segments with varying moments of learning need. Once you make these leaps, the other shifts are easy (Figure 4-4).

Figure 4-4. Summary of Mindset Changes With OK-LCD Model for the Learn Action

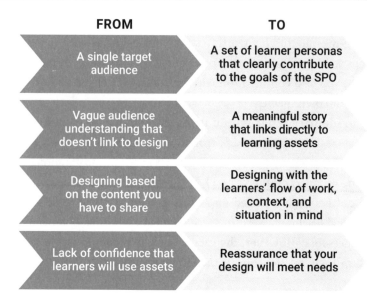

FROM	TO
A single target audience	A set of learner personas that clearly contribute to the goals of the SPO
Vague audience understanding that doesn't link to design	A meaningful story that links directly to learning assets
Designing based on the content you have to share	Designing with the learners' flow of work, context, and situation in mind
Lack of confidence that learners will use assets	Reassurance that your design will meet needs

Throughout the Learn Action, keep your goal in mind: to design a set of learning assets that will meet the business KPIs and on-the-job behavior targets, as outlined in your strategic learning objective. Rather than stopping at a target audience defined by statistics and a few demographics, you want to get the critical data that leads to ideas for meaningful learning assets. And as you proceed to the next Actions, keep these learner personas front and center to drive learner-centric solutions!

The power of the Learn Action is that by understanding the mindset of your learners, you are more likely to attract them and meet their learning needs with your learning products. Your work on the learner personas is the answer to the question, "Why do we think this design will work?"

In Practice

Loc Nguyen, L&D leader from Bluescape Software, completely transformed the approach for his company's software training when he began using learner personas. Like many training professionals, they had fallen into the trap of defining the audience based on what's important to the designer, not the learner. "Fundamentally, we had always thought of learners as: There's a brand-new user, an intermediate user, and a Bluescape expert," Nguyen says. The focus as always was on the level of product knowledge.

As they applied the OK-LCD model for the first time, they considered the on-the-job performance they were trying to achieve *for the learners*. It quickly became apparent that skill level was quite irrelevant.

"Previously, we hadn't looked at it based on their roles and it turns out, different skill levels don't always matter," Nguyen says. "You simply have to be empowered to consume information if, say, you're an executive. And if you're an administrative person, you should really know how to configure permissions. It had little to do with whether or not you're a beginner or an expert."

After redefining the personas based on role and desired behavior on the job, Nguyen and his L&D team began to select and design learning assets. Now, the common questions his team asks are:

- Why are you creating this?
- When will the customers see it?
- Will the customer even run into this content?
- What are they going to get out of it?

"We're really placing ourselves in the learners' position and saying, *Hey, if I were here encountering this particular situation, what could I do with this [learning asset]?* They now will have this entire repository of content that's delivered in various ways accessible to them," Nguyen says. "That's powerful because if you can enable a learner to realize that they have all this available to them, they're going to feel as if they're empowered to learn whenever they need to. *And* the content is going to be palatable to their situation."

Because of the work on learner personas, the front face of the Bluescape learning platform changed. "Instead of going in and seeing a section for a beginning, intermediate, or advanced training, you now see producer, presenter, and consumer," Nguyen says. "You click that icon that leads you to the assets that are most applicable to that function within the Bluescape ecosystem."

As an unintended benefit of the persona work, buy-in for the learning cluster that Nguyen and the L&D team presented was even easier. It was immediately clear how the new approach would benefit and be used by customers. Loc's team member John Quinn says, "I think one of the reasons it was an easy win when we presented these personas at our sales kickoff was because it just made sense [with] the way people use it. Everyone was able to connect with those personas being built out."

Because the learning cluster work has produced such a high-quality product, Loc's leadership team is considering turning the learning assets into a new product for Bluescape. Because the training, in this case, is for external customers, rather than sharing it for free, they believe there's an opportunity to grow their business.

Bluescape's example demonstrates the impact and power of personas. The influence of learner personas spreads all the way from better design ideas, to gaining more sponsorship, and, most important, to a greater positive impact on the learners. However, it's vital to use personas in the context of the full model. Without the on-the-job behavior insight from the strategic performance objective, Loc and his team couldn't have come to the powerful conclusions that they did. Creating personas alone doesn't get you there. Personas are most effective when used in conjunction with the strategic performance objective, as well as the rest of the Owens-Kadakia Learning Cluster Design model, as we will see in the next chapters.

Final Note

In this chapter, we showed how L&D needs to make an essential shift: from analyzing a single target audience to developing multiple learner personas. By having learner personas that relate to considerations important to L&D, we get the data needed to drive the design of multiple learning assets.

To create the best learning experiences for our learners, we need to dig deeper into understanding their mindset and their context, just as a good marketer might do. By adopting the philosophy of the Learn Action and adding the Learn Tool to your toolbox, like Loc and Sravani, you too will be making an even bigger difference for your learners and your business, as you design and develop learning assets customized for the unique learning-moment needs of your personas.

Reflect

◊ What does the analysis of your target audience look like today? What do you like about the process? When adopting the OK-LCD model and the Learn Action, what do you think will be different?

◊ What will help you the most to put the concept of learner personas into action, as guided by the Learn Learner-to-Learner Differences Action and Tool?

◊ What difference will creating learner personas make to your learning initiatives?

◊ Consider the issues our Common Story characters had at the beginning of the chapter. How can the OK-LCD model make a difference with the following issues?

- Providing multiple learning pathways to support learners.
- Building employee trust in the quality of in-house learning assets.
- Customizing learning assets to more closely target individual learning needs.

Apply

◊ Consider the latest learning initiative you are working on. Take a look at the strategic performance objective you developed at the end of the Change Action. Consider what you know already about your target learner group:

- What do you think some of the overarching categories might be that differentiate your learners?
- What plan might you put in place to gather helpful data about your learner group?
- How could you test the validity of your learner personas and persona stories?

◊ Look at the Learn Learner-to-Learner Differences Tool in the appendix or head to LearningClusterDesign.com/Book-Bonus. Fill out each section for a current or recent project to gain deeper practice and insights.

5

Getting a Quick Start!
Upgrade Existing Assets

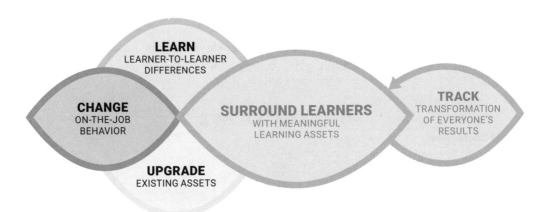

A common approach to modernizing L&D is to throw out what you have and start from scratch. An alternative approach is to introduce new, modern learning assets, while allowing older programs to clutter up your library. In this chapter, we describe a faster approach: Upgrade Existing Assets. This Action reuses and modernizes existing critical or highly visible learning programs by selectively integrating some of the nine elements we describe in this chapter. Harnessing past efforts enables quick, visible progress on modernizing so there is more time for the other Actions.

Organizations can create and collect a large number of training classes and e-learning courses that, over time, can become dated— maybe it's an unexciting delivery, dated graphics, static content, or simply a boring design—because there weren't so many technology options five or 10 years ago.

UPGRADE
EXISTING ASSETS

Recall from chapter 1 our discussion that some training departments have approached modernizing with a "rigid" or "back to core" mentality. Often, the task to modernize seems so daunting that training departments just continue to deliver the learning assets as is—and continue to get the same unhappy ratings and perception from their organizations.

Alternatively, some organizations have a "jump on the bandwagon" mindset. They invest in every new technology that comes their way and just add it to an existing library of programs, leaving it to employees to filter through the mess. One employee described it as being led to a warehouse full of great training, only to find that there are no lights, and he had just a flashlight to help him find what he needed.

Yet training organizations don't have to fall into either of these categories. The Upgrade Existing Assets Action provides a strategy to help you bring a learning program into the future and insights that will lead right into the Surround Action, discussed in chapter 6.

In this chapter, you will become familiar with the Upgrade Action, the nine elements of modern-ness, and the implementation process to bring this Action to life.

A Common L&D Story

Cast of Characters:

CHRO	CLO	L&D Manager	L&D Manager	L&D Employee
Chris	Marissa	Digital Design	Training Delivery	Elaina
		Jon	Ruby	

The Scene: Marissa is having her weekly team meeting with Jon and Ruby just after receiving another request from the CHRO for an L&D modernization budget proposal. She has grown frustrated.

"Chris is once again asking for our learning modernization plan and budget," Marissa said to Jon and Ruby. "Continuing to tell her that our plate is full is simply no longer an option. It's time for us to figure out our strategy to make it happen."

"We just bought the new LMS," Jon said. "We're launching that next month along with the new portal, 'For You University.' Isn't that enough?"

"And we've entered all of our compliance e-learning training and core development classes into the LMS," Ruby added. "It will look really modern when each employee can go online to see their own personalized list of required and elective courses."

"Keep in mind how many courses and classes are in our LMS database. It's huge!" Jon exclaimed. "It represents over a decade of L&D course development. We need to be choiceful about which ones we modernize. We can't do it all overnight!" he said, a bit exasperated.

"I agree," Marissa replied. "We must carefully select which ones to upgrade so we aren't overwhelmed with work. And everyone on our team has done a great job on the LMS implementation. It will help address employees' requests for more training and development opportunities, which comes up repeatedly in exit interviews and employee surveys. But just showing them a list of all the courses available to them—I doubt that is going to change employee attitudes about L&D programs and the development opportunities at our company. Employee ratings are below our benchmark on the end-of-class surveys for about 40 percent of our e-learning courses and 25 percent of our classroom programs. I asked Elaina to do an analysis for me, and based on her findings, a majority of employees feel that our training courses are boring, out of date, or don't help them succeed on the job."

"So, what do we do?" asked Jon, his voice betraying some panic. "Do we scrap everything and start over? That's not realistic."

"And what does it mean to modernize?" Ruby asked. "What does a modern class look like?"

Marissa sighed, overwhelmed. "I don't know. And yet, even our own staff senses it. They want to be part of something modern. They're forwarding emails to me suggesting that we add this new app or that new tech solution. There are so many options. I'm not sure which ones are worth the effort and the money. And I don't want to scrap what we have and start building from scratch. There's good stuff listed in that LMS that I, for one, don't want to lose. I just don't know how to bring our current training programs into the 21st century."

The Issues: How can the OK-LCD model make a difference for Marissa, Jon, and Ruby? As you explore this chapter, form your own opinion on how to address these main issues:

- How do we take on L&D modernization challenges when staffing is already spread too thin?
- How do we handle the backlog of low-rated and business-critical courses waiting to be modernized?
- How do we choose tech options when there are so many choices?
- How do we meet employees' and senior leaders' need for something modern right now?

The Action Explained

This Action is about updating the learning assets you already have by adding just a few of the nine elements commonly present in modern learning materials. In this section, we introduce the nine elements (Figure 5-1) and provide some insights for each.

Learning assets that are infused with today's technology or a digital technology mindset are fundamentally more relevant, engaging, and modern. Yet it's unproductive to simply throw tech—and money—at every learning asset. It's deeper than that. Which technology? How many technologies? What about learners who like face-to-face classes, books, and other traditional forms of learning?

Through our research—searching online and surveying both college and corporate learners—we sought out what learners look for in a modern learning asset. Our findings resulted in the list of nine elements commonly seen in modern learning assets, as shown in Figure 5-1.

Figure 5-1. Nine Elements Commonly Seen in Modern Learning Assets

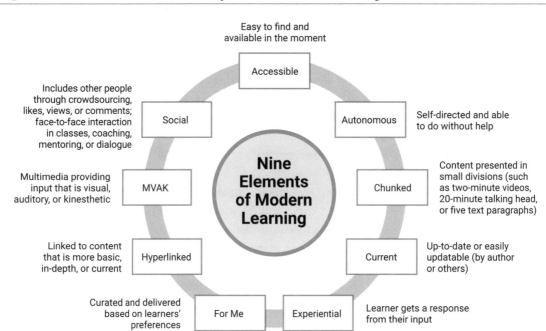

Rather than prescribing particular technologies to modernize existing programs, these nine elements outline the characteristics to look for in any modernization design, regardless of adding online or offline tools. This is powerful because specific technologies may become quickly outdated. Rather than prescribing what technologies L&D needs to include, it's more important to focus on the expectations and benefits learners in a digital age seek. Then you can select modernizing technologies that match the desired benefit, rather than simply chase after the next new tech. And much later on, when that technology becomes dated, you'll be able to select a new one that meets similar needs. Our objective for modernization: Meet learner expectations and provide an engaging learning experience.

The Nine Elements

The **Accessibility** element is about improving how quickly learners can find the information or learning asset. It shouldn't take a 10-minute search to find what is needed. While periodically offered classes are not accessible, e-learning courses can be. However, even e-learning can be made more accessible. Consider these factors that slow down the learners: Do they need manager approval to access the e-learning course? Does it require users to hit "next, next, next . . ." to get to the right screen, instead of having a navigable menu structure? The assessibility element is hard to achieve for secure industries—banking, finance, healthcare, or top-secret government work. It's also hard to achieve for businesses where regulations strictly control when, where, and how employees can work or learn. So, if this element is too difficult to deliver, do what you can and emphasize other elements.

The **Autonomous** element is all about the learners doing it on their own. It might be an e-learning course, a book, or a website. Do not confuse doing it on their own with doing it by themselves. While autonomous often means self-study, it can also include providing chat rooms or a publicly available list of experts to contact for additional one-on-one help. An emerging technology in this space is chatbots for learning. (See Artificial Intelligence and the Nine Elements, later in this chapter, for more on AI and its use in learning.) And simply going location-free with learning doesn't make it effective. According to Moore's Transactional Distance learning theory, which explores distance education, as the level of interaction between teacher and learner decreases, learner autonomy must increase (Giossos et al. 2009). A key to this element is enabling the learner to be in control, while providing a pathway to learn in small-enough chunks to focus on exactly what is needed in the moment.

The **Chunked** element is all about giving people just enough to meet the immediate need. One aspect of chunked is time. How small is small enough? Videos of one to three minutes are great for most instructions. Twenty to 60 minutes is acceptable for in-depth learning, provided there is a way to bookmark where the users left off so they can return to that spot after an interruption. For reading, a paragraph is chunked. A page is getting long, but is more easily digestible if it has graphics to more quickly convey and reinforce the text. One aspect of the Ebbinghaus Forgetting Curve research reinforces the need to have small bites that can be reviewed frequently as needed.

Another aspect of chunking is how content is segmented. The chunked element doesn't require that all learning assets must be short. Immersive experiences are a part of the future. For example, from high-school students learning biology to corporate trainees mastering complex soft skills such as negotiation and decision making, virtual reality offers an immersive, distraction-free learning environment. When focused on a well-chunked enabling objective, such experiences are highly engaging. We will return to VR in the Surround Action in chapter 6 as we talk about options for modern learning assets in a learning cluster. For face-to-face classes, there is wide variation in chunking content as well. If you've got a five-day new hire program, look at ways to divide the material into effective part-day sessions. Research shows that learners can only take in so much in a day in an efficient way. Give them just what they need in order to learn without wasting time.

To be **Current** often means that there is a method for updating the content on the fly. In-class trainers can do this easily, simply by noticing that something changed and telling class participants about the change, thereby increasing the trainers' credibility by confirming that they themselves are up-to-date. For other learning assets, give users confidence that it's up-to-date by using systems that allow for changes. For example, with online materials, add or use systems that allow users to comment. A simple way to get started is to add a footer telling users how to contact the content owner if the user notices something out of date. For a more advanced example, picture how Wikipedia works versus the old *Encyclopedia Britannica*. Rather than having a single owner, systems like Wikipedia democratize update capability and rely on the crowd to fact-check and maintain quality. Not only does this approach help L&D organizations with limited resources, but imagine how this feature connects the L&D department to experts they didn't know about within their own company! As someone from the Pentagon put it to us, "We know there's someone somewhere in this building with the skill and the ideas—their team might think they are crazy—but we just don't know where they are sitting!"

The **Experiential** element is about users getting different responses based on an action they do during a learning experience. An in-class role play or table discussion qualifies. So does an Excel spreadsheet or e-learning course that accepts an answer or entry and delivers a result or response. Clicking "next, next, next . . . " in an e-learning course does not qualify. A multiple-choice answer that provides insights into the choice (right answer, or wrong answer with explanation) is a step in the right direction. Did you know that through machine learning and VR capabilities, modern learning assets can create a "choose your own adventure" approach for learners? These programs create a unique learning path based on their correct or incorrect responses.

The **For Me** element is what LMSs often do so well. Users can log in and see exactly what courses they must take and what is available on the topics they have an interest in. Yet we can and need to go further. Learners want their learning pathway to be curated for them, not to be given a list of everything L&D has to offer. In addition, so many L&D departments have to deliver so much compliance training that the development training never gets entered into the mix. If this is true where you work, think about how to change the situation. Can a learner set up their LMS profile to indicate topics of interest to them so they get alerts when new content is added? Alternatively, can those employees with an expressed interest be tapped to write a few one-pagers on the topic that can be shared with other employees via the LMS, a curated blog, or other learning pages?

Hyperlinks make everything easier. The key is to provide links to both prerequisite information and expanded or more advanced information. By providing both, learners can either get up to speed on prerequisite content, or explore the topic further based on their preferences and time constraints at the moment of learning. Good hyperlinks will open in a separate window or have some other mechanism to easily get back to where the user started. But watch out for broken hyperlinks. It can be very frustrating for learners. An error such as "This page cannot be found" is a fast way to quell anyone's desire to try to learn more. Be sure you have a system for ensuring that links are up-to-date and functioning.

MVAK is all about multimedia, including visual, auditory, and kinetic neural inputs. Currently, audiobooks and podcasts are all the rage for some groups. YouTube is the go-to learning tool for other learner groups—but don't forget interactive infographics, as well as the huge potential of video game and VR environments to deliver a multimedia experience. What might your learners like? What would best serve the strategic performance objective? For example, would watching an interaction be more valuable than listening to the steps to take for soft-skill development? You can create multimedia from existing content in several ways. Besides hiring a multimedia designer, try assigning learners a small portion of an existing class to convert to a video or audio file. That serves several purposes—it reinforces learning for the learner, helps learners feel involved and engaged beyond their normal job, and helps L&D crowdsource some learning assets that others can use in the future. Crowdsourcing is a great way to give L&D modernization a helping hand.

The **Social** element has several layers. *Social* means people. Modern learners want to interact with other people, because dialogue may help them learn and expand their perspective. They want to hear what others have to say on a topic, and they want to validate the experts' information by gathering opinions from others. They gain insights from their peers as well as from SMEs. Sometimes social comes in the form of face-to-face group interaction. Other times it's about getting perspective from the community by reading comments and recommendations about a course, blog, book, or video. Even the number of thumbs-up and thumbs-down on a stand-alone learning asset can provide social insights for learners. Social can also be accomplished by creating an infrastructure to connect individuals with a question or problem to individuals who are likely to have an answer. This might be a mentoring program or an "Ask the Expert" system.

Artificial Intelligence and the Nine Elements

Artificial intelligence is no longer a distant dream. Its adoption is happening at an accelerated rate, and we can expect AI in learning to emerge in many ways, if it hasn't already in your organization. Driven by the data source it has been programmed to store, AI gives machines the ability to recognize, respond to, and learn from inputs (SAS 2019). Three branches of AI are primarily available: natural language processing, computer vision (image recognition), and voice recognition software. As with each new technology, we should test it against the nine elements to ensure it will serve our learners. AI aligns with many of the elements, and we believe AI can be a valuable addition to our learning assets.

AI drives three of the nine elements—accessibility, for me, and hyperlinked—through features such as "suggested for you." When you use YouTube, suggestions pop up in multiple ways: when you begin to enter a search in the search field, on the homepage from videos you've watched previously, and at the end of a video you just watched. Does your LMS have these capabilities, or are they coming in future upgrades? Now is the time to find out!

AI also empowers autonomy. For common questions that new hires might ask a colleague, a chatbot could be the answer—and more accurate and up-to-date! Or for a new product that's just hit the market, your sales function might upskill more efficiently through interacting with a chatbot, considering their on-the-road travel lifestyle. But remember that a chatbot is only as good as the data it's fed to learn from. If the initial set of answers to FAQs is not comprehensive or the different ways a question could be asked are not considered, users will get frustrated.

Lastly, AI can even empower social learning. AI can help learners create and share their own learning playlists. Colleagues in similar situations don't have to rely on L&D understanding their needs, but can find curated curriculum created by others who are closer to their work. If you haven't already, begin working on upskilling your knowledge on AI and talking to suppliers to understand the possibilities for upgrading your existing assets by including AI.

The Action's Impact

Before jumping into a deeper description of the elements, let's explore the advantages of the Upgrade Action. We see five benefits: Improve learning, create a more positive impression of L&D's products, help L&D explore new technologies on a smaller scale, provide L&D with insights that are useful when you get to the Surround Action, and last but not least—modernize quickly.

First, many of the nine elements are consistent with modern research on the neuroscience of learning and can help you deliver learning assets that further improve performance on the job. Thanks to newer medical technologies, researchers can actually see how the brain reacts more clearly than ever before. Researchers have debunked old theories about maximizing learning by matching learning styles or increasing repetition. We've even learned that our brains do not stop growing at a certain age, and that "old dogs" *can* learn new tricks.

Second, this Action also helps you meet today's learners' expectations and creates a more positive impression of the L&D department's work. Learners, regardless of age or generation or even geographic region, have gotten used to receiving the benefits of digital technology. The majority of the nine elements reflect this shift in expectations.

As an example of this shift in our learners' experiences and expectations, let's look at just one element—accessibility. Long gone are the days when people waited to get their news exclusively from a newspaper delivered to their front porch. Rarely do people drive to the library to peruse the card catalog to find a book to match their research topic. And while people do still drive to stores to shop for clothes, household goods, and groceries, even this has changed. Can't find it? Just order it online and have it shipped to your doorstep. People today expect the benefits of email, shared digital workspaces, and shared calendars. They expect learning opportunities to be more accessible and easily found. Let's strive to match what learners expect so that they are more engaged and open to changing their on-the-job behavior based on what they learn with the modernized learning assets we provide them.

Third, the Upgrade Action gives you the reason and opportunity to explore new technologies on a smaller scale. Perhaps you've been interested in trying out some new tech, but don't want to commit to a big contract with the supplier. Instead, work out a deal to pilot the technology as part of the project to upgrade an existing learning asset in order to improve one particular element. If the technology works well for you, great! If you see multiple programs benefiting from the same upgrade, you can build the business case for intentionally investing more broadly in that new proven technology.

Fourth, the Upgrade Action can give you a jump start on the Surround Action, described in chapter 6. In the process of thinking about ideas for modernization, we've seen L&D professionals brainstorm so many great ideas, but there are more ideas than they can possibly implement in the moment. We tell them, "Don't lose these ideas! Capture them and use them when you get to the Surround Action." It's an energizing way to carry your positive momentum forward.

Finally, upgrading your assets is a fast way to get started on modernization and show the company that L&D still has it! It's like picking the low-hanging fruit. There's no need to reinvent entire classes to achieve this level of modernness. Don't underestimate this value!

Figure 5-2 has some of the changes you will need to make to your mindset and behavior as you shift from traditional instructional design to the OK-LCD model for this Action.

Figure 5-2. Summary of Mindset Changes for the Upgrade Action

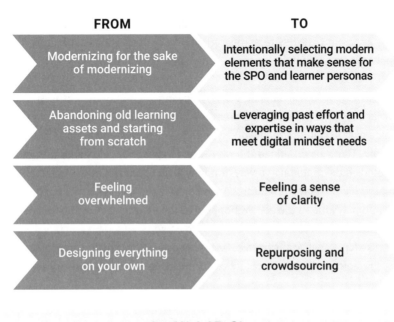

FROM	TO
Modernizing for the sake of modernizing	Intentionally selecting modern elements that make sense for the SPO and learner personas
Abandoning old learning assets and starting from scratch	Leveraging past effort and expertise in ways that meet digital mindset needs
Feeling overwhelmed	Feeling a sense of clarity
Designing everything on your own	Repurposing and crowdsourcing

An OK-LCD Story

Cast of Characters:

| CLO Marissa | L&D Manager Digital Design Jon | L&D Manager Training Delivery Ruby | L&D Employee Edwin |

The Scene: Marissa gets an update from her L&D manager team, Ruby and Jon, on how they will be modernizing a critical existing initiative: the onboarding program.

"We are making good progress on modernizing our onboarding training," Ruby told Marissa. "We're starting by making the section on company history more accessible and autonomous by putting it on our LMS. Jon? Has your team had a chance to load that slideshow yet?"

"It's scheduled for next week," Jon replied. "The audio file had to be converted to a different format to be compatible with the LMS. No problem though. I like how you got your trainers to do a voice-over and captions on the slides. And it contributes to our company's inclusion goals for differently abled populations. Such a simple thing. Won't the new hires be surprised when they recognize their trainer's voice!"

"Ruby, it makes me a little nervous having our history done via self-study," Marissa said. "After all, our history is part of the foundation of our common culture! Shouldn't this be done in person?"

"That's what I was thinking too—at first!" Ruby replied. "Then I got to talking with a few new hires fresh out of the program as a part of my research for the Learn Action on building learner personas. It soon became apparent that they remembered next to nothing about our history. I think we are overwhelming them with content during the in-person session. Chunking this part into smaller bites could help.

"To test my thinking," Ruby continued, "I asked Edwin to run a small test with four new hires. It cost us four lunches and yielded some great results. The instructions are to independently go through the voice-over slides, and then work in pairs to write a two-minute play about an assigned part of the history. That's how I added the MVAK and experiential elements of modern learning. The new hires studied the material in a way that they liked to study. Later, when they watched one another's company history plays, it reinforced the content and it was so much more memorable. I confirmed this informally the next week by stopping by to talk with each of the four new hires about what they remembered. They recalled more than I did on some of the history facts!"

"That sounds like fun, Ruby!" Marissa said. "More importantly, this paired activity directly supports our program's strategic performance objective for building social networking among new hires. Good job!"

Jon had been listening intently. "Sounds like there are some other benefits to this approach too," he said. "We could, with permission, record their plays and repurpose them for other training, with minimal work for us and lots of fun for our employees."

"Crowdsourcing content! Yes! I like it." Marissa exclaimed. "Can you imagine our employees five years from now, sharing a link to their old recording with a new batch of new hires! What fun! And it would reinforce our history yet again. I can't wait to see the improvements in the ratings for the upgraded onboarding training."

The OK-LCD Difference: Because they have the power of the OK-LCD model, the L&D team is able to assemble a clear, data-driven strategy for upgrading existing assets.

The Action Implemented

To role model the OK-LCD model, we provide several ways to help you change your own on-the-job performance as you adopt and implement this way of designing modern learning. So far, you've read about the concepts and benefits of the Upgrade Action. In this section we describe how to do it using a tool created to guide the process for this Action. Figure 5-3 is an image of the tool that you will find full-scale in the appendix as well as LearningClusterDesign.com/Book-Bonus.

Figure 5-3. Upgrade the Existing Tool

Element of Modernness	Rate Existing (1=Yes; 0=No)	Possible to Add? (Y/N)	How to Add It? (List Ideas)	Do It Now or Later? (N/L)	New Rating (1=Yes; 0=No)
Accessible					
Autonomous					
Chunked					
Current					
Experiential					
For Me					
Hyperlinked					
MVAK					
Social					
Total Score					

For each learning asset that you strategically select to modernize, use the Upgrade the Existing Tool as a spreadsheet step-by-step as follows:

1. Evaluate the modernness of your existing learning asset by assigning a point value.
2. Brainstorm modernization ideas for each of the nine elements to be used within the current learning asset or for new additional learning assets.
3. Explore combinations of upgrades using a numerical value to quantify the extent of modernization.
4. Select the modernization ideas you want to implement and rate the new plan for moderness.

Select strategically. Start by intentionally and thoughtfully selecting the learning assets you want to update. Then use the Tool to upgrade them. When selecting a few learning programs that are important to the organization, look for ones that:

- Get low scores on the end-of-program evaluation.
- Trainers complain are not engaging to them or to their learners.
- Are already on the docket for a major content overhaul.

Evaluate modernness. For each asset that you've selected to modernize, the next step is to determine the level of modernness that already exists within the asset. In a few cases, our clients discovered that the program was already significantly modern, and instead, they needed to jump straight into the Surround Action, described in the next chapter.

Use the tool to record your modernness evaluation. For each of the nine elements, add one point if the element is already built in, and zero points if it isn't. Then, add up how many "modernness points" the asset has. If the point value is too low, in your opinion, keep moving forward on this Action. As you do more modernness assessments for a wide variety of learning assets, you'll learn to quickly spot those that need upgrades.

Brainstorm modernization ideas. Individually, or as a team, brainstorm a variety of ways that the existing asset might be modernized. Consider the following questions for each of these nine elements:

- Is it even possible to add this element to your learning asset (yes or no)?
- Would adding this element help the learning experience become more effective? (Add a comment on your thinking.)
- If we added this element, what are the ways we might do it? (Record one or several ideas in the List Ideas column.)

The Upgrade Tool is a great way to capture your thought process. And when you're done, there are usually too many great ideas to implement! That's OK. Save these for possible use during the Surround Action.

Explore combinations. After brainstorming possibilities for all nine elements, select just a few ideas that will:

- Engage your learners (Learn Action).
- Be consistent with your strategic performance objective (Change Action).
- Match your current capability, budget, and schedule.

Often, one or two ideas will show up across several of the elements. For example, the most common, in the early stages of L&D modernization, is to convert a classroom course to an e-learning course, which can be designed to add the elements *chunked*, *MVAK*, and *accessible*. Play around with the combinations, and keep in mind that the goal is to add modern elements to these assets in a way that is meaningful to learners.

Watch out! It may be tempting to try to add all nine elements to each learning asset, but that would be overkill. Selecting just a few of the elements or modernization ideas allows you to focus on the ones that add the most value for the most realistic level of effort.

Assign a new rating. Once you've narrowed down your options, give a name to this combination of added elements, and re-rate the modernness of the asset. Give a score of one for every element the asset now has, and a zero for ones that are still not a part of the design. Do you see a modernization difference? Then, start recreating and modernizing the training. Do not hesitate to test your ideas out on your learners in advance to make sure the final product will indeed increase their engagement with the learning.

Look for patterns. Do the same technologies come up over and over? As you go through multiple upgrade projects, you may discover that a few of the same technologies provide the benefit across several learning assets and modernization projects—technologies that work well for the company's environment, industry, and budget. You may want to invest a bit more in such technologies to encourage greater use to spread the cost. Rather than investing in the latest and greatest technology ad hoc, seeing patterns through applying this Action empowers strategic investments.

These nine elements have always been available to us, but now we can include them with greater ease in a digital age. It's like early television. Because of the habits of producers and show writers, early TV was often more focused on dialogue than the action alone. The nine elements remind us to use new and often already-available tech.

In Practice

Upgrading assets through the nine elements of modern learning is a powerful action. One L&D manager, Greg Goold of Paycor, had a unique approach to getting started immediately. He handed out the list of the nine elements in a department meeting and asked staff to consider how the list could help level up their current projects. The group was energized. For them, the list provided a common language. Rather than feeling overwhelmed by all the possibilities they had read about or seen at conferences, the nine elements made it easy to organize, assess, and brainstorm new ideas for their programs.

An OK-LCD Story

Cast of Characters:

CLO
Marissa

L&D Manager
Digital Design
Jon

L&D Manager
Training Delivery
Ruby

The Scene: The L&D team discusses the modernness of blended learning programs and what improvements can be made.

"Hey, Marissa," Ruby called out. "I wanted to get your opinion on something Jon and I have been debating. Do we really have to modernize our blended learning programs? After all, I feel like we already chunked the material by splitting it into self-study prework, then the class, and then follow-up. And the online component is autonomous and accessible because we tell them to bookmark the link when they sign up for class. Plus, it's social when we get the class together. Isn't that good enough?"

"It depends," Marissa replied. "What are your Kirkpatrick Level 1 evaluations telling you? If the learners are giving you scores that meet our benchmark—80 percent on a 100-point scale, or a 4 for those organizations using the 5-point scale—then let it go. The priority is on those programs that are underperforming."

Ruby looked pleased. "Good! That sure will save a lot of work. You're kind of saying, 'Don't fix it if it isn't broken.'"

"Yes, and I would like to challenge you on two of your definitions—for *accessible* and *chunked*," Marissa said. "As we move forward, let's try to set up systems that don't require our learners and users to remember to bookmark a website or save our email with the link. We want to streamline this so our learners can spend their time learning and doing the job that they were hired to do."

"Makes sense. Maybe we can add some hyperlinks to the LMS landing page for the course. After all, we are trying to drive the behavior to use the LMS weekly, if not daily, for every learning need. What's your concern about *chunked*?" Ruby asked.

"From what I'm reading in the literature, chunked learning is much smaller than an hour-long e-learning course or one-day class. I'll leave it to you and Jon to see what you can do to break it down further. Our employees often need just a one-minute reminder or a short two-sentence tip to meet their on-the-job needs. Let's see if our course materials can be chunked that small so that, after the course, the pieces can be reused as stand-alone learning assets on the job. Reusing and repurposing what we've already created will really save time and money for our department. Plus, I think our learners will appreciate it once we make it easily accessible and part of their daily habit of learning," Marissa explained.

"Makes sense; we will look into it!" Ruby replied.

The OK-LCD Difference: Focusing on what is important to the business and our learners is key to helping L&D set our priorities as we modernize. Our previous blended learning designs were a step in the right direction toward modernizing, and we can take it to the next step with a learning cluster design.

Final Note

In this chapter, you learned how much easier it is to upgrade existing assets and create a modernization plan when you have the key characteristics, or nine elements, of modern learning in hand to guide the process. When you complete the Upgrade Existing Assets Action, double check to ensure that all the pieces fit together. Here's a helpful checklist:

- Add a few of the nine elements to upgrade the learning assets.
- Confirm that the upgrade is engaging and motivating for each learner persona.
- Confirm that the upgrade choices align with the strategic performance objective.
- Save a list of the extra ideas to update the learning asset so these can be used in the Surround Learners With Meaningful Learning Assets Action, described in chapter 6.

Consider this: Many of us were attracted to the L&D and HR industry because we enjoy working with people. Technology may not be in our wheelhouse. Yet L&D has a habit of adopting technologies—from film strips, slide projectors, overhead projectors, PowerPoint, CD-ROMs, and DVDs to, in more recent years, e-learning, websites, and multiple versions of LMS systems. While it may seem difficult for us to integrate the latest technology into our learning programs, L&D as an industry has a history of doing so successfully.

What makes this next set of technology integrations more difficult today is that there have been so many changes in such a short period of time. It's overwhelming! By using the list of nine elements, we can focus on what our learners need: the benefits they—and we—desire from technology integration. With renewed focus, we can move forward more quickly. With the nine elements, we can move forward with confidence.

Reflect

◊ Consider the issues our Common Story characters had at the beginning of the chapter. How can the OK-LCD model make a difference for Marissa, Jon, and Ruby on the following issues?
  - Staffing is spread too thin to take on the challenge of modernizing L&D.
  - There is a backlog of low-rated or business-critical courses waiting to be modernized.
  - It's hard to select tech options when there are so many choices.
  - Employees and senior leaders want something modern right now.

◊ Name at least one technology that supports each of the nine elements (Figure 5-3). Are these technologies things you already do at home or at work?

◊ Consider which of the nine elements you prefer, and why. How will you find out what your learners prefer?

◊ We often think our modernization work is done because we have blended learning, a new technology, or the latest fad. How can the nine elements expand your team's ideas about modern learning?

◊ What could be the consequences of skipping or skimming the Upgrade Action? How does the Upgrade Action of the OK-LCD model empower L&D to strategically upgrade existing assets?

Apply

◊ Consider a recent learning initiative you worked on. If you were to apply the nine elements, what might your modernized program look like?

- Given unlimited funding and resources, how would you include more of each element in your L&D program? (Reminder: Add just a few elements to each modernized learning asset.)
- Considering what's possible in the short term with the budget you have, which ideas could you execute in the near term?
- How could you leverage the concepts of reuse, repurpose, and crowdsource to accelerate your work?

◊ Take a look at the Upgrade Tool included in the appendix or visit LearningClusterDesign.com/Book-Bonus. Fill out each section to gain deeper practice in the Upgrade Existing Assets Action.

6

Surrounding Learners in Their Moments of Learning Need

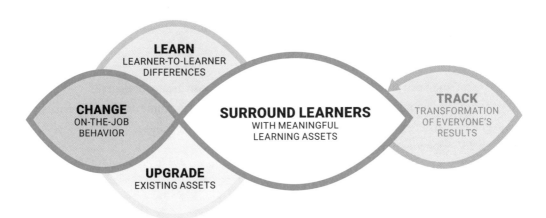

In an age of continuous change, we need continuous learning. The best learning experiences need to be available in the formal arena and where our learners work, in times and situations of their choosing. In the Surround Learners With Meaningful Learning Assets Action, we create a learning cluster made up of strategically selected assets. This strategy builds upon the earlier Actions as L&D selects assets by taking into account three things: the desired behavior change outlined in the Change Action, the learner needs as identified in the Learn Action, and the availability of learning assets at the three learning touchpoints—social, formal, and immediate. This strategy propels L&D toward learner-centric, performance-driven solutions for today's modern learner.

Employees typically have limited choices for learning at work:

- Take a classroom class.
- Take an e-learning course.
- Do blended learning—some individual study plus a class and an assessment.
- Talk to someone they know at work.
- Ask their manager.
- Read instructions or SOPs or a handbook.
- Get approved for an external class.

SURROUND LEARNERS
WITH MEANINGFUL
LEARNING ASSETS

Outside work, employees have more options for learning, and they use them successfully, even without guidance from learning specialists:

- Ask others—blogs, chat rooms, and so forth.
- Watch videos—TED talks, YouTube.
- Get hands-on experience—volunteer or join a group.
- Go to a local university—for a degree, a certificate, or just an evening class.
- Learn from friends and family—near and far, phone or online.
- Peruse wikis –Wikipedia, WikiHow.
- Read books and guidebooks—online or the library.
- Sign up for an online university or a MOOC—for a class, certificate, or degree.
- Try online do-it-yourself searches—Google Scholar, newsfeeds, some academic journals.
- Use guided learning programs—books, online, local groups, or colleges.
- Watch TV—documentaries, movies, educational shows.

Figure 6-1. When Modern Learners Engage

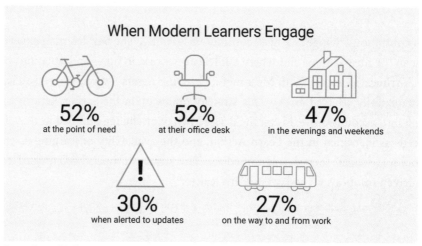

Source: Greany (2018).

It's time for L&D to close the gap. Why? Because employees expect it, and because our businesses need employees to learn even faster and deeper in this rapidly changing environment. With today's technology, L&D can go beyond formal learning and begin to support unplanned intentional learning.

Yet L&D is holding back—the task seems overwhelming! Moving beyond formal instruction is historically outside L&D's sphere. For years, forward-looking L&D professionals have tried to move us outside our classes by encouraging us to shift to "performance support," to get learning materials into the workplace where learners need them. Unfortunately, our industry is often defined narrowly as being responsible for training, and performance support is considered a distant, second goal in importance. Training limits us by defining the product we are expected to create, rather than the result we are trying to achieve. Fortunately, we've come to see ourselves as responsible for learning.

By claiming the title *learning and development professionals*, we open new doors, and it's time to step through them. Let's take our learning assets out into the workplace to the people who need to learn. Let's not simply wait for them to come by and take our training. Let's surround them with meaningful learning assets, designed to be readily available when, where, and how people need to learn. How? This Action—Surround Learners With Meaningful Learning Assets—is the key to your strategy to meet the modern learners' needs.

In this chapter, we'll explain this Action, which is the focal point of all the others.

A Common L&D Story

Cast of Characters

| Employee Jaik | Employee Ana | Employee Nina | Employee Nick |

Scene: Jaik discusses having to take training with his co-workers Ana, Nina, and Nick.

"Hi, Jaik." Ana waved as she approached him in the hallway. "Ready for lunch?" Jaik nodded, but kept walking. "What's going on?" Ana asked as she caught up with him.

"I just had my quarterly performance review today with Julia," Jaik replied.

"How did it go? I mean, you were expecting a good review, weren't you?" said Ana. "What happened?"

"Oh, it went fine," Jaik replied. "There's just one issue. Our project has been running behind schedule, and Julia holds me partially responsible. Of course, she's uptight with everybody on the team right now. So, it's not just me. But she said that my project management skills suck and I'd better improve. Said that her mentor warned her that the entire C-suite is 'focused' on our project and we have to look good. She wants me to get ahead of the game and start fixing this right now."

"You always were her favorite. She wants to get you fast-tracked for advancement," Ana said encouragingly. "So why are you so down about this? It doesn't sound like they're going to fire you or demote you or anything."

"She told me to get some training. Told me to look it up on the company learning university site. I did. I hate going to training classes!" Jaik replied with frustration.

"There's Nina and everybody," Ana said, waving. "Tell me more over lunch." Later, as their group sat down at their usual table, she restarted the conversation. "Jaik's been told to take some project management training. He doesn't want to go. Tell them about it, Jaik."

"Bummer," Nick said.

"Lucky guy!" Nina retorted. "Wish I could get a free day off away from the day-to-day grind."

"Well, it's a two-day class," Jaik explained. "I think this is the one Andy went to last year. He told me it was OK. When I called him just before lunch to ask about it, he said that he hasn't looked at any of the project management stuff since the class. What a waste of time! And if the company is all worried about us getting projects out the door, they shouldn't waste our time sending us to project management classes. They should let us spend all our time doing our work!"

"I tend to forget what I do in a class," Nick admitted. "Even if I take notes. I'm better off with a book, so I can read a bit each day, underline stuff, take notes in the margins, and grab the book when I forget stuff."

"Book!?" laughed Nina. "I'd rather have e-learning. That way I can cover a few slides at a time, in between interruptions. But what I really like is the e-learning that I can download and take on my commute. Plus, if the online training lets me bookmark pages, I can take a quick look to remind myself before going into a situation. The conflict management training was like that."

"As far as I'm concerned," Ana said, "I'd like to figure out how to get Alexa to just whisper in my ear to remind me when I'm trying to form a new habit. That would be the best. It would be like having a personal guru or coach 24/7."

Jaik grinned. "Next thing you'll be asking for is a brain implant to replace training classes!" They all laughed and agreed that the world was changing and they were fine with that.

The Issues: How could the OK-LCD model and the use of learning clusters better meet the differing needs of Jaik, Ana, Nina, and Nick? As you explore this chapter, form your own opinion on how this Action addresses these main issues:

- How do we manage differing attitudes toward classroom learning?
- How can we improve recall a few months after training?
- How can we meet differing needs for fitting learning into employees' schedules?

The Action Explained

In this fourth Action, you create the learning cluster that, when designed thoughtfully based on the data collected in previous Actions, will surround learners with the learning assets they need to improve performance in a particular area.

Typically, L&D needs to cram every bit of content into the one class when we have the learners' attention, because we likely won't get their attention again. The business wants the performance fixed now, one-and-done. How difficult for us and for the learners!

Recall in chapter 2 that we defined today's modern learner as someone who needs to learn fast in an ever-changing environment, and who will access a wide variety of resources to get answers. Our learners have so many moments when they need to learn. Just consider the Mosher and Gottfredson Five Moments of Learning Need model:

- learning for the first time (new)
- learning more (more)
- applying what you've learned (apply)
- when things go wrong (problem solving)
- when things change (change).

L&D overwhelmingly focuses on the *new* moment of learning need. And, L&D focuses exclusively on formal learning. Now, with the OK-LCD model, we have a way to teach business leaders to expect something different—rather than a training class or course, we can give them a learning cluster.

In this Action, we decide how to pull apart that big ball of one-and-done training into meaningful learning chunks, new chunks that weren't possible in the event-based world, and figure out how to get all these different chunks in front of the learners when, where, and how they are most likely to need them. Knowing which assets make sense for the whole is where the work lies. Each asset should work together to promote the strategic performance objective for the learning cluster. Unlike traditional ID models that design single assets that lack alignment with other assets, learning cluster design focuses on designing the whole, not just the parts.

Designing a learning cluster involves an intentional, context-centered approach to selecting, designing, and facilitating access to a set of learning assets to improve performance on the job for a particular capability.

A New Concept: Learning Touchpoints

The idea of learning touchpoints, which comes from business and marketing, encourages us to look at all those instances when the learners can come into contact with learning content. This is a new concept for most L&D professionals, and an essential component to select the best learning assets for the learning cluster. To keep it simple, we broadly categorized three types of learning interactions (social, formal, and immediate), based on neuroscience research on how people learn. In each interaction between the learner and L&D, we are sending a message of what we think will help the learner most, given their persona and the strategic performance objective.

L&D has traditionally focused exclusively on the formal learning touchpoint—face-to-face or virtual instructor-led training, blended learning or e-learning. What research shows is that learners use these formal learning products, on average, only once a quarter (Degreed 2016)! Today, our learning assets are not a big part of their life. What learners crave are products that provide a mix of social, formal, and immediate touchpoints. Learning clusters should have at least one learning asset in each of these three touchpoints, tailored to each learner persona.

Social Learning Touchpoint

This is an instance of learning in which learners have a level of interaction with other people. What learners seek from a social touchpoint is either interactions with others to help them learn, or validation from others about the veracity of the content, especially as it applies to the learners' context. Instructor-led training—classes and virtual—typically provide this for learners. And it is easy to layer on another level of social interaction by allowing users or readers to add their ratings and comments. Social commenting is commonly seen on video sites, wikis, blogs, learning asset listings (such as training catalogs), chat rooms, and posted articles. Ratings and comments are a powerful way to help learners understand the relevance of a learning asset for their context.

Depending on the SPO and the performance gap, you may want more or fewer assets in the social learning touchpoint, but for every persona there should be a social learning opportunity. Learners seek the richness of the interaction beyond the trainer or SME alone. Get creative. Outside of work, people engage in social learning through new platforms all the time. Beyond YouTube comments and likes, there are websites like Twitch, which allow live chat during practicing a skill, or Coursera, which leverages discussion boards as a part of learning. Consider including even such simple things as desk drops, posters, and cafeteria table "did you know" tents to get the social interaction going on critical performance topics.

Formal Learning Touchpoint

This is an instance of learning in which learners experience a clear start and end point, and a structured sequence or path to follow, often ending with a completion certificate. Modern learners do crave formal programs. What they most often seek are foundational immersive learning, recognition, completion satisfaction, interactions, personal development, authorized time to focus on a skill, and insights through a broader, trusted network. L&D most often reaches learners with formal touchpoints. These are structured, with the least amount of learner-choice on what to learn and who to learn from. Formal training can be in person, but it can also be an e-learning or a blended learning program. The key is that in formal touchpoints, learners follow a predefined sequence through content or engage in experiences with a clear start and end point. Smart L&D professionals do everything they can to make these exciting or fulfilling. It might be adding a badging program for compliance training, or a desirable certification for completion of elective learning programs or building in networking opportunities across the inevitable company silos. Or it might be simply adding fun stuff!

Immediate Learning Touchpoint

This is an instance of learning in which learners' experiences include 24/7 access and availability in the moment, without extensive searching. When learners need to learn, they often can't wait for the scheduled class, or for permission to take an online course, or even to find someone who can help with their questions. They need to know now! That is where immediate learning touchpoints come in. Typically, this type of asset is online in the form of job aids, wikis, searchable databases, active discussion boards, or menu-driven, bite-size e-learning content. This touchpoint includes all assets that the learner can access independently. Your role in this touchpoint is to create assets that can be used in this way and to facilitate easy access to these assets. You might not even know whether these assets are used or in what sequence they are used. This is commonly an underused touchpoint with few learning assets, or it is overused, but learning assets are difficult to find. Your job is to populate more assets in this touchpoint so learners don't have to rely on external content that may not have the quality or content needed to fill their gap. Your second job is to guide access to these assets, often by partnering with IT or external suppliers to create more streamlined platforms with better search algorithms.

Figure 6-2 offers a summary of the three learning touchpoints, examples of learning assets for each touchpoint, and learning assets that overlap into multiple touchpoints.

Figure 6-2. Three Learning Touchpoints

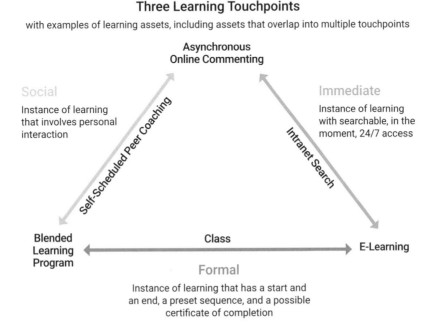

When you consider these three learning touchpoints, the 70-20-10 learning model might come to mind. This model says that 70 percent of learning occurs through working, 20 percent through working together, and 10 percent through formal training (Jennings, Heijnen, Arets 2019). The 70-20-10 model is another approach that has encouraged L&D to consider their role outside formal learning. However, in practice, organizations inadvertently make the following mistakes:

- Believing that 70-20-10 is a prescription—learning assets must follow this exact ratio.
- Shedding accountability—L&D is only responsible for the 10 percent part of the ratio.
- Limiting the kinds of learning assets and learning moments—70-20-10 is often simplified to on-the-job, coaching, and classroom as the learning asset types, excluding other moments of learning.

In contrast, the concept and language of learning touchpoints is not prescriptive, emphasizes L&D accountability, and allows easy inclusion of emerging technologies. For example, learning via podcast doesn't quite align with any of the 70-20-10 categories, but for OK-LCD, it easily falls into the immediate learning touchpoint. The breadth implied by the three learning touchpoints encourages L&D to explore and include new learning assets for today's technology and tomorrow.

In Practice

The Gorilla Glue Company was expanding. It needed to onboard more people, upskill staff, and promote more employees than ever. LuAnn Tarvin and Brienne Crouse, the organization's L&D team, smartly surveyed leadership on what they needed. The response was typical—a laundry list of training topics narrowed to 78 that management wanted within the year. At the owner's suggestion, they brought in one of the authors as a consultant to help with this massive task.

In partnership with IT, they created their own version of a learning cluster page, showing the calendar of upcoming training events as well as a curated set of resources for building skills on these topics. Resources under each skill area were categorized as "Read," "Watch," "Attend," or "Do." All learning assets were linked for easy access. Employees quickly saw that at the Gorilla Glue Company, they could learn with or without a formal course—it's their choice.

Additionally, to ensure employees invest time in their learning goals, L&D sends out the monthly training event calendar with a WHYLL reminder: What have you learned lately? When the email goes out, there is a distinct uptick in hits on the learning cluster page. With prompts and support from L&D, employees and leaders alike are learning to be part of a continuous learning culture.

Introducing this learning cluster format and regular reminders to use it has resulted in several changes. At first there were several requests for formal training classes, but after month three, the requests from managers changed. Instead of "Can you do a class on xyz?" it became "I have this problem. What can you do to help solve it?" Instead of spending time teaching classes, the L&D team members spend time applying their skill set to solving company problems. And by involving other employees in the problem solving, they're able to position these instances as employee-learning projects. Here are just a few examples of how they are continuing to build the learning culture and the learner experience:

Problem 1: Limited Contractor Understanding of Work

Contractors are regularly brought in to production to help with peak-capacity orders. Leadership indicated that the contractors didn't seem to have a strong understanding of the work. The result: high turnover and frustrated line leads, who are responsible for contractor training. L&D's innovative idea was to create very short pre-employment videos for contractors. They got the line leads involved in the video scripting and recording for the four common contractor assignments. Videos highlight the process flow, safety, performance expectations, and the department's value to the organization. Contractors are more eager and confident to start work, and line leads are even more energized by their contribution to this learning project, which has had a big impact for themselves and the company.

Problem 2: Inconsistent On-the-Job Training Within Logistics

Leaders in Logistics were receiving feedback that on-the-job training was inconsistent between different trainers in the department. L&D worked with the team to create a comprehensive training checklist, which included cross-training opportunities to promote even more consistent training.

Problem 3: Team Leaders Operating in Silos

Despite team leaders participating in a monthly roundtable, there was still a disconnect between different departments and shifts. They were operating in their own silos instead of as a full production team. When asked to help solve the problem, L&D put their needs analysis skills to work. Their solution was to add an "assignment" component to the cross-representation roundtable program. Having assignments gave these employees a clearer purpose for being on the team, as well as a more active role in developing relationships with other team leads across different areas and opportunities for additional learning and development on problem solving, team building, and cross-functional capabilities.

The Gorilla Glue Company's L&D successes have given the team additional excitement and momentum that will lead to other resources, solutions, and opportunities for employees.

Implementing the Action

This is the action where we roll up our sleeves and start putting the learning cluster design philosophy to work to create the learning cluster. To ensure we don't just jump in and design a single training program, we need to take a different path. Instead of starting with content analysis and learning objectives for each asset as we do in traditional ID models, we first ensure that we are creating a learner-centered, modern solution. We choose and design learning assets that match when, where, and how people need to learn to deliver improved performance and drive the KPI and on-the-job behavior change outlined in the SPO. In this section, based on the Surround Tool, we will describe how three of the Actions feed into this Surround Action, then walk through the various steps to create your own learning cluster design, and finally, build out the objectives hierarchy envisioned in the Change Action.

Use Previous Actions to Prepare

With the OK-LCD model, the Change, Learn, and Upgrade Actions provide insights that guide and influence this Surround Action. Here's how:

- **Start with name and strategic performance objective.** Give your learning cluster a name. Typically, it's named after the skill or performance that it will improve, like "the Feedback Learning Cluster" or "Accurate Records Learning Cluster." Then jot down your strategic performance objective so it is front and center in everyone's mind throughout the process. The SPO represents the goal of the learning cluster.
- **Recall learning asset ideas.** In both the Learn Action and the Upgrade Action, you would have noted learning assets that might be good for a specific learner persona or for this specific learning cluster. You also may already have modernized existing learning assets—these will become a part of your learning cluster as well. Gather those ideas to get ready for the next step.

Develop the Learning Cluster

The process of forming a learning cluster uses a guided innovation technique of diverging (brainstorming), mapping, converging, and checking (Figure 6-3).

Figure 6-3. Learning Cluster Development: Guided Innovation Technique

Diverge/Brainstorm

Starting with the learning asset ideas you gathered, consider each learner persona, one by one, and brainstorm learning assets that have potential for meeting their unique needs. Consider the learning experience for each persona:

- Will they have what they need when they need it for all five moments of learning need: when they learn the first time, learn more, apply, troubleshoot, and deal with change?
- Is it clear where to find small chunks for remedial or advanced learning help?

- What is the reality learners will experience when implementing the capability back on the job? How closely can the learning experience mimic that reality?
- What barriers does each key persona have to overcome to achieve the strategic performance objective? What learning assets can help the most?

For easy reference, it's helpful to name learning asset ideas, typically based on the media or method of delivery, such as conflict video, situation analysis e-learning, speaking from principles self-analysis. Add a high-level description of the content and learning objectives that are likely to be addressed by this asset. At this point, be open-minded, and unlimited by budget, timing, and current infrastructure. Don't hesitate to test out your holistic ideas about learning assets on a few learners to gain additional insights or to confirm that you are on the right track.

Converge

Now it's time to look at all the learning assets that you identified and select those that are realistic for your situation and that most broadly meet the needs of your learners when they strive to achieve the strategic performance objective. Here are some ideas to help with your selections:

- **Repurposing.** Look for multipurpose assets that meet the needs of several personas. For example, a one-pager on a topic could be used during a learning activity in a class, as an immediate job aid online, or as pre-reading for a webinar. Reusing and repurposing reduces your L&D workload.
- **Chunking.** Because different personas need to learn different things to be able to perform the goals in the SPO, the design team must ensure that the combined learning assets cover all the needed learning objectives for each persona. But this needs to be balanced with the modern learning design rule: "Teach only what they don't know." Assets can be chunked so learners can skip what they already know. One way to accomplish this is to start with the lowest-skilled persona and determine everything they need to close the performance gap. Then, with all those learning objectives and learning assets, chunk it—into remedial assets, core assets, or advanced assets—so each persona can get just what they need.
- **Leveraging scale.** Maybe there are technologies that you don't have now, but that would serve a large portion of personas' learning needs. Maybe it's an updated LMS, chat system, blog software, leaders-as-teachers approach, or mentoring program. This is the time to go to bat for them. Additionally, tap into company infrastructure wherever possible. For example, does the company have any wikis or shared-site technologies? Is there a regular newsletter or homepage where L&D could post content to drive spaced learning? This is a good time to strengthen your relationship with other parts of the company and justify new technology initiatives.

Map

Next, categorize the learning assets, both by persona and by the three learning touchpoints: social, formal, and immediate. The goal is to ensure that each persona has at least one learning asset at each touchpoint—that all bases are covered. If not, back up to brainstorming again and consider what would meet the learner persona need at this touchpoint.

Many of these assets will cover multiple touchpoints. That's good! For example, a class is likely social and formal; e-learning is formal and may be immediate (if available whenever desired and the content is menus-driven, not a next-button format); and a chat room is social and immediate. Learners need each touchpoint, but to varying degrees, dependent on all those things you learned while developing learner personas.

The Surround Tool has a visually helpful Venn diagram that supports mapping across multiple dimensions (Figure 6-4). The diagram shows the touchpoints and the learning assets, each assigned to a persona. The blocks are movable and replaceable. It's like using a floor plan app to figure out how to place furniture in a room; it helps you see what fits and where the gaps are.

Figure 6-4. Excerpt From the Surround Tool

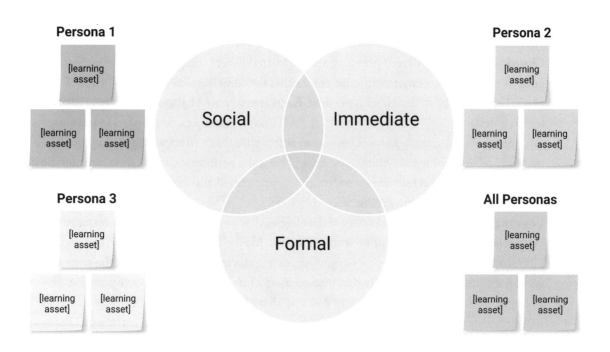

Check and Recheck

While the stepwise process for developing a learning cluster—Diverge, Map, Converge, and Check—sounds linear, as with most creative processes, as new ideas are uncovered, there is some iterative looping. This final check encourages such iteration; checking and rechecking is a hallmark of instructional design. These three checks are crucial:

- Do you have a learning asset for each learning touchpoint for each key persona?
- Are there any needs uncovered from your learner personas that are not being met?
- Do the assets further the strategic performance objective for your learning cluster?

Align Learning Objectives to Learning Assets

Return to the Change Action and the hierarchical relationship of objectives. Map the multiple layers of terminal and enabling objectives using the following process:

1. Start with the learner persona with the lowest skill level. Determine what they need to close the performance gap.
2. Map those objectives to the learning assets that are most likely to be used by that neediest learner.
3. Looking at the other personas, identify what they need in addition, and, more important, what these other personas don't need.
4. Pull bits and pieces from the neediest-learner assets into other assets to meet the needs of the other learners. Chunking and reusing chunks is a big part of this work.

To keep it modern, apply the principle, "We teach only what they don't already know." The key to delivering on this philosophy is to identify the learning chunks that are needed by more than 80 percent of the people who are likely to use that learning asset. If the chunk is needed by less than 20 percent of learners, that material—be it content, activity, or experience—is spun off into a remedial learning asset. It might be a hyperlink, a "for more, see xyz," or a test or assessment that selects the shortest learning path through the available learning assets.

And don't hesitate to add connections to advanced learning assets for those who want more. Watch out for signs of too many options, which research shows can cause people to reject all the options because choosing is difficult. We don't want to smother our learners, only surround them with meaningful learning assets. Having three to five learning assets per learner persona is a good target.

When you're done, list your final set of terminal objectives and enabling objectives. Indicate which learning assets will cover each objective.

Design Each Asset

Once you have your final learning cluster and you've jotted down the terminal and enabling objectives, the detailed development of each asset begins. Designing each of the various assets in a learning cluster is no different from your normal design and development process. You can use your organization's favorite ID model, because the traditional ID model's goal is to design a single learning asset. You will find that a lot of the data you've collected in the OK-LCD model will be reapplied as you develop each asset.

The Action's Impact

Designing learning clusters instead of classes and courses is the answer to so many of the "wish fors" for L&D professionals. We wish we could:

- Stop cramming everything into one training.
- Find ways to reinforce learning periodically after training is complete.
- Space learning over time for better retention for our learners.
- Reach learners when they want and need to learn.
- Have a strategy for integrating new technologies into training.

The learning cluster does all of these.

Instead of all assets being classes and courses, now we have a mix. Maybe it's videos, self-study guides, links to reading materials laid out in a helpful outline format, or a self-assessment program, wiki, or chat room. Maybe you've added a "question of the day" reminder program, or a learner experience online or face-to-face.

Regardless of what assets you choose for a learning cluster, you can now look for patterns. What new tech might meet a wide variety of needs for many of your learning cluster projects? What infrastructure could you begin building with a learning cluster and reuse it for many more to come? Perhaps it's setting up a culture of "Thursday Thoughts" (13 minutes of thoughts and reflections on Thursdays on what was learned this week, typed into a database that is either private or shared with managers and mentors). Perhaps this is your opportunity to get buy-in for L&D to make good use of the company systems for video, shared sites, blogs, communities of practice, or other common work apps and programs. Each year L&D should be adding something to the mix, while replacing things that have become dated over time, with the goal of both meeting needs and driving higher engagement.

Just keep in mind that we're not about tech for tech's sake, but we do want to provide meaningful learning assets that meet the learners' needs and the strategic performance objective. The In Practice story shows how learning clusters have worked at one company.

In Practice

Paycor believes "in good technology, good deeds and in the goodwill of our clients. It's not just business, it's personal. We're our clients' partner, our coworker's friend and the community's ally." And Paycor has been growing quickly, with many opportunities for advancement every day. But the rate of growth is outstripping the speed at which they are developing the next leaders.

Greg Goold is the company's director of talent development and learning. He pulled together a team to design a learning cluster called Aspiring Leaders Learning Path to support the company's need for more promotable leaders, and employees' desire for high levels of responsibility. According to Goold, "The objective is to develop an awareness of the critical capabilities necessary to be successful as a people leader at Paycor. Developing skill in these critical capabilities is not the objective. Because the work of a people manager is often done out of the sight of the direct reports, it is necessary to increase the awareness of these leadership capabilities in individual contributors who aspire to people leadership. This allows them to begin to seek opportunities to develop those capabilities both prior to, and after becoming a people leader."

When first looking at the target audience, the L&D team lumped everyone together as "aspiring managers." However, on closer evaluation, they identified three groups. There was Self-Selected Sandy, who wanted to be a manager in the near future but did not currently have a manager mentor. Then there was Recommended Robin, whose manager mentor was encouraging her to move toward a leadership role. The third group was Midcareer Matt, who was a highly skilled individual contributor. If Midcareer Matt could master more of the people-management skills, he could help the company by augmenting group management as needed, or he could discover that a management role would match his interests after all. Too-Soon Taylor aspired to be a manager but was at least two years away from this being a realistic goal. It was hard to know what to do with Too-Soon Taylor, but Paycor would lose this enthusiastic employee if left unattended.

And while all learner personas were ready and willing to learn, their learning needs drove them to different learning assets, as shown in Figure 6-5.

This learning cluster affords people the opportunity to choose how to learn, then bring their learning to class for deep, rich discussions, where they can share their thinking and get comments from experienced managers. Based on the after-class evaluations, the Paycor culture is only getting stronger through this program. The participants appreciate the curated resources, and Paycor curation gives them confidence that this material is in line with Paycor's culture and the critical capabilities for Paycor leaders.

According to Greg, "Another advantage of the learning cluster approach is that we aren't totally ignoring the Too-Soon Taylors at Paycor. While it will be several years before this learner is qualified for the program, Taylor can still search any materials tagged on the website as 'Aspiring Leaders Learning Path' and use many of the resources that the program participants use for their group sessions and monthly assignments. When the time is right, Taylor will be more than ready to participate."

Greg described the results to date: "We are on our fourth cohort in 18 months, and the results are already positive. We are pleased to be delivering on our strategic performance objective.

"On our promote-from-within goal: We had a goal of supporting promotions from within. While 11 percent of attendees were designated HiPo, and slated for promotion, 15 percent of those who completed the aspiring managers course have been promoted in this short period of time. We expect the numbers to continue to climb.

"On our higher employee engagement goal: Employee engagement scores average 11 percent higher for managers who have attended the aspiring manager training program. Further, on

the coaching index score (annual assessment of managers completed by their direct reports), managers who attended Aspiring Manager score 5 percent higher than managers who have not attended.

"Our goal for on-the-job behavior change was to increase discussions on these core managerial skills among peers and mentees. Qualitatively, we are getting stories—both voluntary and from select follow-up interviews—that participants greatly appreciate how the aspiring manager program expanded their network, and that they now have someone outside of their immediate work group to talk to about the core managerial skills—their successes, problems, evolving perspective. They are getting and giving peer coaching on Paycor's core managerial competencies."

The OK-LCD Difference: For Paycor, using a learning cluster design enabled them to building managerial capability with spaced learning that empowered these employees to learn when, where, and how they wanted to learn. Everyone is benefiting!

Figure 6-5. Excerpt of the Surround Tool for Paycor's Emerging Leaders

1. **Name of Learning Cluster:** Aspiring Leaders
2. **SPO (Change Action):** By improving core managerial skills (see list attached) for employees with the potential and desire to become managers, the business will benefit by having more promote-from-within managers and higher employee engagement as these aspiring managers rise through the ranks. (KPI measures: annual engagement survey and "coaching index," which reflects employee's perspective of their manager.) The changes to on-the-job behavior that we will see among aspiring managers include application of the core managerial skills, and discussions among peers and mentees on these core managerial skills.
3. **Learning Asset Types by Learner Personas (from Learn Action and Upgrade Action):**

Self-Selected Sandy*	Recommended Robin (HiPo)*	Midcareer Matt*
Classes (web or face-to-face), e-learning, blogs, job aid downloads	Mentor, classes (web or face-to-face), video library, web link to success stories	Higher-level mentor; lead panel discussion (learn by doing)

*All personas include those at headquarters and those in remote locations. All learning assets must treat both local and remote equally.

Additional persona: Too Soon Taylor. Taylor wants to be a manager and wants to get ahead of the competition by starting now with managerial education. While Taylor is not the focus of this learning cluster, all the immediate assets are available to Taylor. Current managers are being told to direct Taylors to these resources to prevent shutting down their enthusiasm.

4. Learning Cluster Development

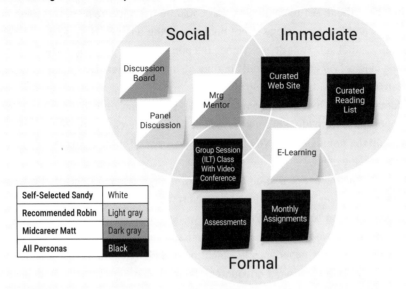

Self-Selected Sandy	White
Recommended Robin	Light gray
Midcareer Matt	Dark gray
All Personas	Black

Learning Assets	Description and Comments
Assessment	Online assessment to identify current strengths and development opportunities related to management competencies (requires debrief)
Curated Website	Items listed by monthly topic, including articles, job aids, and videos
Discussion Board	LMS chat feature for discussion of assignments prior to group sessions; often facilitated by Midcareer Matt (who gets training on facilitation)
E-Learning	E-learning courses, related to monthly topic, available through LMS
Group Session (face-to-face plus video conference)	Monthly session of all participants to discuss one of 16 monthly topics and assignments (small-group activity uses phone for one-to-one participant interaction to include remote participants)
Manager Mentor	Current manager who has completed manager development training, assigned to each aspiring manager participant; for Matt, higher-level manager
Monthly Assignment	Complete assignment questions and case studies; includes suggested learning assets to assist aspiring managers in finishing assignment
Panel Discussions	Panel of current managers with strength or experience in the monthly topic area to share their experience and answer participant questions
Curated Reading List	Online curated reading list of management development content

Future Technology

In L&D, we often hear about the latest technologies that could be used for training. Wrapping an entire class or course around one technology is not necessarily the answer. How do we try new tech, or fit it into our current tool set? How do we choose the purpose and design of the technology for a particular learning cluster? As you read about Foundry 45 and virtual reality, consider it within the context of one learning asset within a learning cluster.

Foundry 45, an Atlanta-based virtual reality company, works with organizations large and small to bring VR learning opportunities to life. Let's take a look at several use cases for VR in learning. These use cases highlight the range of ways VR can be used to meet different terminal objectives for learning assets in a learning cluster:

- **Technical "how-to" objectives:** For a large shipping company, Foundry 45 created a warehouse VR experience, training "pickers" on the line to sort packages appropriately.
- **Soft skill or critical thinking objectives:** Foundry 45 works on complex capabilities as well as leadership or crucial conversation skills. For these capabilities, a VR experience acts as a "choose your own adventure" experience in which the real-life environment surrounds the learner, including the people they might encounter. The learner is confronted with dialogue from characters and must choose how to respond. Based on data provided by the client of best-in-class and worst-in-class responses, the software knows the ideal path to navigate the situation, and the learner is guided and tested appropriately.
- **Awareness objectives:** For clients like Delta Airlines, Foundry 45 has created live scenarios to familiarize people with the environment of a plane on an airport tarmac.
- **Knowledge check objectives:** For all types of scenarios, whether through practicing a skill, taking a test, pointing at objects in the environment, or navigating a conversation well, there's a way to test if the learner really "got" it.

How do you decide how to use a tool like VR in your company? In old L&D thinking, we might have approached VR as a one-trick wonder—many of us see only one possible application of the tool—in the VR case, it's often seen as a how-to simulation for technical skills. However, with the power of the OK-LCD model, we put ourselves firmly in the on-the-job reality of the learner. We can create the right asset for the right moment of learning need, and tailor our tools as needed to fit. Now, a tool like VR could be used in anything from onboarding to negotiations to operations. Our work on learner personas, strategic performance objectives, and learning touchpoints guide us to ensure new technologies like VR have the right learning guidance behind them.

While these people are experts in software, they are not experts in L&D. Companies like Foundry 45 are trying to reinvent the instructional design wheel. They are trying to understand how to design a learning experience, and they are seeking the right data from their clients. But guess what? We in L&D are their clients! Many of us in L&D can get intimidated by new technologies, but with new IT and supplier partnerships, we can focus on our expertise, and bring the future to our organizations. As we in L&D level up our capability for the digital age, we can make sure new technologies are strategically designed to make an impact!

Final Note

With the Surround Action, you now have the power to deliver modern learning to your organization. Every Action has built upon and reinforced one another to design the ideal learning cluster to close the performance gap.

In the past, you might have delivered one asset, or directed learners to many different places to get assets that weren't uniquely designed for them. Now you are able to deliver a set of learning assets selected strategically with your learners in mind, with a clear targets outlined in the strategic performance objective. At this point, it might sound like a monumental task! But you're not alone in creating this new world. As we detail in chapter 9, we have a suite of learning assets to help support you—from other ways to learn the OK-LCD model to expert consultant help to deliver your next project. For now, make sure to take a moment and review the Reflect and Apply questions to integrate what you've learned so far.

You now have a way of thinking and a way of doing modern learning design that improves on-the-job performance and elevates L&D's contribution to the organization. All we need is to measure it! And the next chapter, the Track Transformation Action, will give us what we need to be able to tell an impactful story about our work.

Reflect

◊ Can you think of a past learning design that included materials that went beyond the class or course? Maybe it was a job aid or an improvement training program to be completed with the learner's manager. How was this similar or different from a learning cluster? If a learning cluster were the norm at that time, how would that make a difference in the way the materials were received, used, or even designed?

◊ What one or two ideas from this chapter empower you to put the Surround Action into practice to create learning clusters?

◊ What will the learner experience feel like when learning clusters are in place for every topic?

◊ Consider the issues our Common L&D Story characters had at the beginning of this chapter. How can the OK-LCD model make a difference for Jaik, Ana, Nina, and Nick in terms of:
- opposite attitudes toward classroom learning
- poor recall a few months after training
- differing needs for fitting learning into their schedule?

Apply

◊ Consider a recent learning initiative you worked on. If you were to convert it to a learning cluster, what might you change to accomplish the following:

- better meet learner-to-learner differences (research might be needed to spot differences)
- put assets into the workplace so learners are surrounded by meaningful learning assets
- chunk materials differently, and reuse or repurpose chunks multiple times
- test a new tech tool that you've had your eye on?

◊ Take a look at the Surround Tool in the appendix or download the latest version at LearningClusterDesign.com/Book-Bonus. Fill out each section to gain deeper practice in learning cluster design.

7

Measuring Transformation, Not Just Participation

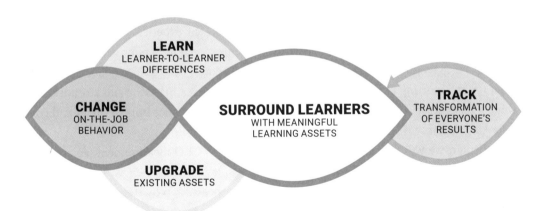

In an age where concepts like big data are front and center, L&D measures evolve by moving from measuring participation to measuring transformation. In the Track Action, select measures that indicate progress on the desired on-the-job behavior and KPI changes, as defined by the Change Action. This is how you will confirm that the learning cluster is working for everyone—learners, the business, and even L&D. With these data, L&D shifts from providing the standard backward-looking report card, to providing leading data that the business and L&D can use for continuing transformation.

With the Track Transformation of Everyone's Results Action, C-level leaders stop asking the backward-looking question:

TRACK
TRANSFORMATION
OF EVERYONE'S
RESULTS

"Is the money we spend on L&D worth it?"

and start asking the forward-thinking question:

"What is the data telling us we need to conquer next to meet talent needs?"

Today, whether we are talking about online or offline learning, we in L&D most often report learner usage and reaction. We measure how many people use a particular platform or have completed a particular course or class. We measure satisfaction through end-of-class "smile sheets" or the "Like" button next to online course offerings. Yet, as emphasized in the Change Action (in chapter 3), where you put your focus is where you are going to go. When it comes to measures, is focusing on learner *reaction* and *usage* where we want to go? If we tell our leaders and employees that this is what L&D contributes to the enterprise, will they appreciate and value our work?

By putting focus on usage and reaction, we are saying that what's important is the volume of people who use our products and their feelings about the in-the-moment experience. Of course, after many years of seeing such data, this is exactly the data that organizational leaders now expect. But what do we learn about business impact from such metrics? In this Action, L&D shifts the focus to on-the-job transformation by reporting changes both in KPIs and in employee behavior and attitudes. By doing so, we share a fuller story about what's important: sustained performance improvement and collecting forward-looking data that will help shape future learning initiatives.

In this chapter, we will first look at a different approach to L&D measurement, an approach that tracks transformation for everyone—learners, the business, and L&D. Then we'll discuss the Track Tool, which helps break down the measurement selection process, step by step. Finally, we'll describe changes in our measurement approach that can shape the modern learning approach.

A Common L&D Story

Cast of Characters:

CEO
Doug

CHRO
Chris

CLO
Marissa

CFO
Marc

CMO
Raj

The Scene: The leadership team has gathered for its regular meeting. Today's agenda includes the HR year-end report and budget request for next year.

"Next up on the agenda is the HR report," Doug said to the leadership team. "Chris, you're up!"

"Thanks, Doug," Chris said. "As you know, HR is composed of several departments. I've invited the leaders of each department to join us and tell you their plans for the upcoming year. First up is Marissa from Learning and Development. Marissa?"

"Thanks, Chris. Thank you all for giving me the opportunity to share the great work we are doing in L&D," Marissa said as the L&D score card was handed out. "As you can see from our scorecard, we are on track for every measure. We look at how many employees we serve, the efficiency of our training development process, and the efficiency of the training we provide based on employee ratings, tests, and usage."

Scorecard for L&D: September 2019–August 2020

Item	Measure	Change YTD	On Track	Comments
Serving Employees (Averages per Full-Time Employee)				
training cost	$520	+2%	yes	inflation 1.91%
hours of training/year/employee	32 hrs	−5%	yes	varies ±8% per year
% compliance training done	83%	+2%	yes	goal is >80%
% pass first time compliance	60%	+8%	yes	goal is improve by 5%
% competency training	21%	+2%	yes	goal is >20%
% of employees trained	89%	+2%	yes	goal is >80%
Efficiency of Training Projects				
cost saving	$9,000 saved	n/a	yes	reduce external instructors
new training project costs	in budget	n/a	yes	
new training on time (avg)	80% on time	+10%	yes	staff added to make target
Effectiveness of Training				
student class ratings (avg)	82%	+0.5%	yes	goal is >80% for classes
student test scores (avg)	84%	1.3%	yes	compliance training only
compliance training complete	87%	85%	yes	DB accounts for 4%
hours of classroom instructions	1,000 hrs	+52 hrs	yes	formal training only
# e-learning used	187 programs	+14%	yes	out of 205 available
% using leadership e-learning	35%	+9%	yes	no data for previous year
# e-learning completed	37%	n/a	yes	no data for previous year

Marc interrupted. "Marissa, it's great to see that you have met all your goals. And it's nice that you saved some cash by pulling the training instructors from in-house versus external suppliers. But I have to ask, what is the overall value we're getting for the budget you have? Your operating budget is relatively stable, and the annual project budget is based on the projects that the leadership team requests or agrees to do. Can you give us a sense of what we are getting for that money?"

"Now let's be fair here, Marc," said Raj, trying to take the heat off Marissa. "For one, we get new hire training that my new hires require. Without that, recruiting couldn't get anyone to accept our offers."

"Plus," Chris joined in, "there is a huge cost avoidance of fines from government agencies if we did not have the compliance training in place and someone who can pull the training stats for auditors."

"OK, I get it," Marc relented. "But you can't blame your CFO for wanting a few more hard-core numbers. And, Chris, when I see that employees average an 84 percent score on compliance training, that concerns me. Shouldn't they be getting it 100 percent correct every time?"

The conversation devolved and got off track. Chris called time so the next department could present. She asked Marissa to work with her on a memo to address the concerns raised in the meeting. Later, Marissa told her team, "I got through the C-suite meeting. It went about the same as most years. Chris will do a good job of protecting our budget, as she has always done."

The Issues: How can the OK-LCD model make a difference for Marissa and Chris? As you explore this chapter, form your own opinion on how to help L&D prevent some of the awkward concerns and questions raised in this C-suite meeting:

- Are L&D goals meaningful to leadership?
- Why does L&D's worth come up repeatedly, even though leaders intuitively recognize the impact and necessity of having a learning function?
- How can L&D become a competitive advantage for the company, instead of simply reacting to C-suite requests?

The Action Explained

Recall from the Change Action in chapter 3 how we in L&D have been constricted in defining our goals because we've limited ourselves to what can be accomplished by the end of a course. While L&D has long attempted to measure business impact and ROI, it has been difficult to measure. After all, how would anyone know if one particular learning asset had sustained impact on performance on the job? Trying to isolate the impact of a single program is one reason many L&D teams give up on tracking transformation. With the OK-LCD model, it's time to make another go of it. The Track Action is about new measurement thinking, made possible with learning clusters; using measures to report L&D's impact; measuring the combined effect of multiple learning assets; and choosing measures that are relevant for the three learning touchpoints.

The New Possibility With Learning Clusters

By delivering learning clusters with learning assets that meet the many moments of learning need, we have shortened the distance between L&D's work and employee application on the job. This reduces the unpredictability of what happens after learners leave the classroom (Figure 7-1). Now, with the broader scope of learning clusters, we can have more confidence that L&D products are affecting performance on the job. However, by increasing the number of learning assets in our product line, the number of possible measures also increases. We need to be intentional about what measures we track so that we can report an accurate, meaningful picture of the impact of a learning cluster without being buried in data.

Figure 7-1. Reducing the Unpredictability of Measuring Impact

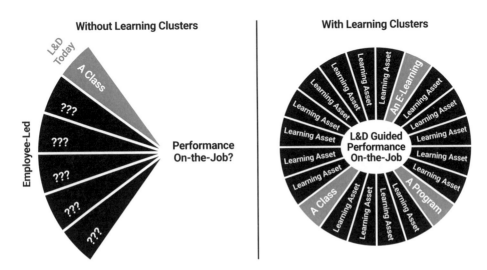

The Track Action is about selecting measures for a learning cluster that track the transformation we set out to achieve, as captured in the strategic performance objective. To track transformation in an impactful way, consider the main reasons measures are important. Powerful measures can:

- **Articulate meaningful targets** so learners, L&D, and the business know the "finish line" that they are currently shooting for (KPIs, on-the-job behaviors).
- **Demonstrate value** that invites further support through funding and resources.
- **Spread awareness** of the learning cluster and its availability to learners.
- **Provide internal feedback** so L&D knows what is working for learners and what needs improvement.

There's no doubt metrics are important. Now we need to figure out how to make them work for us.

Emphasizing Metrics That Show and Tell Transformation

One of the key principles behind the OK-LCD model is to change on-the-job behavior. When starting on the Track Action, review the Change Action, which describes the desired behaviors and business metrics for the learning cluster. For those of you familiar with Kirkpatrick's Levels of Evaluation (see the sidebar for a quick refresh), you might notice the consistency between OK-LCD philosophy on measures and the Kirkpatrick Levels. In our experience, L&D struggles for resources because the value isn't clear. That's why our emphasis in the Track Action is to measure and report Kirkpatrick's Level 3 and 4. These are the data that the business cares about the most!

But our measures may fall short if we don't build awareness. First, learners must be aware that the learning cluster exists. Be sure to create a marketing plan or system so that employees will use your products. Confirm that your plan or system works by measuring awareness of the learning cluster. Next, ensure that users of your products know that the product comes to them through L&D. Every learning cluster, every learning asset, and every L&D system should have L&D's logo or brandmark on it. L&D can then include metrics like Net Promoter Score (NPS) to gain the customer perspective on our L&D products.

NPS is based on research by Frederick Reichheld and Bain, which found that a single question is most effective in understanding customer loyalty: "How likely are you to recommend xyz to another?" (Reichheld 2003). While NPS doesn't tell you why or what to do about unsatisfactory scores, high NPS scores indicate viral enthusiasm about a product, so much so that many would be willing to stake their personal reputation on the value of a product. This is an idea worth reapplying for our learning clusters. Just by reporting good NPS, we gain traction and awareness that can help spread transformation.

Finally, to meet the need of feedback for improvement to L&D, and to meet base expectations of measurement, Level 1 and 2 should still be tracked. However, the primary focus is on metrics that reflect performance change across the target learner groups, and on the resulting business impact.

Kirkpatrick's Levels of Evaluation

In 1960, Don Kirkpatrick proposed four levels for the evaluation of training that are very useful for the L&D industry. The four levels are:

- **Level 1: Reaction.** The degree to which [learners] find the [learning asset] favorable, engaging, and relevant to their jobs.
- **Level 2: Learning.** The degree to which [learners] acquire the intended knowledge, skills, attitude, confidence, and commitment based on their participation in the [learning asset].
- **Level 3: Behavior (or Application).** The degree to which [learners] apply what they learned during training [or through use of the learning asset] when they are back on the job.
- **Level 4: Results (or Impact).** The degree to which targeted outcomes occur as a result of the training and the support and accountability package [or as a result of the learning cluster].

Other methodologies have built on Kirkpatrick's work. For example, Phillips's ROI Methodology adds two other levels: Level 0—which measures the number of training programs and attendees, audience, costs, and efficiencies—and Level 5, ROI, which compares monetary benefits with the costs of the program.

Measuring the Combined Effect of Multiple Assets

When it comes to measurement, a key difference between the OK-LCD model and past models is that the Track Action considers the impact of multiple learning assets that are organized into a learning cluster. This is something very new for L&D. Existing methodologies are strictly focused on evaluating one learning asset, and, in practice, only formal learning assets. OK-LCD practitioners measure Level 3 and 4—Behavior and Results—at the overall learning cluster level, instead of the individual learning asset level. This is absolutely critical.

In the past, L&D's success or failure was often reliant on usage of a single learning asset. If people were not using that asset, it might be removed, updated, or left collecting dust. In the learning cluster world, however, L&D designs assets knowing that everyone will not use each asset equally! That was intentional, as part of our work in the Learn Action. Now, instead of seeing low usage as a failure on the part of L&D, we celebrate the ability to meet nuanced learner needs by reporting the success of the full learning cluster instead. But, we can still remove assets if they aren't working. Metrics like NPS and Kirkpatrick Levels 1 and 2 tell us if an asset is meeting a persona need or not, and if its inclusion in the learning cluster needs to be reviewed.

Choosing the Right Metric for Each Learning Touchpoint

This Action highlights how Reaction, Learning, and Behavior measures may manifest differently depending on if the learning asset is a social, formal, or immediate learning touchpoint. For example, we know from the neuroscience of learning and the AGES model that emotion has a lot to do with learning. Consider how the emotions of a learner might be different during a coaching call with a peer versus covering the same topic in an e-learning course. When it comes to learning assets that belong to the three different learning touchpoints, what you measure and how you measure it could look very different. As you measure these differences, you will discover what works well for your learner personas to drive the desired behavior.

Here's an example. Consider a YouTube-like video as an immediate learning asset. How could we evaluate its effectiveness at the Application level? The metric could be as simple as asking if the learner was able to complete the task at hand after watching the YouTube video. Alternatively, you could measure whether the learner had to seek out additional materials to achieve success. In this case, one metric could be to directly ask the learner: "Was this video all you needed to complete your task?" Another method would be to use background analytics to indirectly measure and track how many people stop the video early, or move on to another asset, instead of completing the video and getting back to the work task at hand.

This same how-to situation could look very different in a social or formal learning situation. For example, at the end of a class, you might only be able to measure the Learning level. You might use a knowledge check or a practice simulation to see if learners can complete the task on their own. The metric is simply reporting how many people pass the knowledge check or complete the simulation. An alternative for in-class activities is to ask the trainer to complete an after-class evaluation. Ask such questions as, "In your opinion, did at least 80 percent of participants demonstrate competency during the in-class activity?"

Finally, look for measures that track L&D efficiency and effectiveness. For example, a simple number-of-hits measure on a reading asset can provide clues about user preferences, as well as needs for L&D to increase awareness that a learning asset exists. If no one is clicking a learning asset, and you have confirmed awareness through other means, maybe it's time for L&D to reduce their own workload by eliminating assets like this. A caution: Don't drop a learning asset type just because only 10 percent of learners use an asset. It's highly possible that those 10 percent of learners really value and need this asset. Keep this in mind as you design your measures so you can get the full picture of what your learners want and need to enable them to learn and behave in a way that drives results.

When you complete this fifth and final Action, you will have selected the measures and systems you will be tracking, so that you can begin to Track the Transformation of Everyone's Results: L&D, your learners, and your business!

The OK-LCD Story Continues

Cast of Characters:

CLO
Marissa

CEO
Doug

CHRO
Chris

L&D Manager
Digital Design
Jon

The Scene: Jon just shared his proposal for a learning cluster for compliance, including new measures. Marissa is giving him feedback.

"I'm liking this new learning cluster approach for compliance training, Jon," Marissa said after hearing his proposal. "In particular, I like how you are planning out the measures. Let me try to summarize what you are proposing to do differently. Tell me if I've got this right:

"First, everything is now tracked on our upgraded LMS. Our dashboard shows what percentage of employees—and managers—are behind on completing compliance tests. Monthly reports flag issues that we can follow up on. Measures are no longer a once-a-year event, after the fact, when it is too late to intervene and make improvements.

"Second, you added some learning assets that fall outside of the formal compliance e-learning course and the related test. These would reach learners at the immediate and social learning touchpoints. I can see how these would provide spaced learning throughout the year, in between the annual e-learning course and the test. I'm particularly fond of your 'compliance story of the month' concept. Soliciting stories from across all the employees, internal auditors, and managers can provide great insights for all of us. These stories are a different form of measurement: a qualitative measure that says behavior change is happening.

"Third, you have added some measures—the thumbs-up and comments feature for the video bites, and online job aids—to indicate if employees are finding these materials, and if employees think they are useful.

"Lastly, you are suggesting we get the internal audit scores, by department, and correlate these to the percent on-time completion of compliance training, and to the percentage of correct scores on the compliance tests. This may provide leverage for getting some recalcitrant organizations to get compliant. I suspect that the numbers will reflect better audit scores for those organizations that have a higher percentage of employees who use the training."

Jon nodded. "You've got it! I'd like to experiment this first year with a few other measures, especially for the overall impact of the learning cluster. But that's most of it. It feels good to be able to go beyond the once-a-year 'compliance mill' that everyone in the industry seems to be doing, and provide support for employees so that compliance training is more user friendly."

The OK-LCD Difference: By completing the Track Action, Jon was able to suggest measures that showcase the fuller story of the learning cluster's impact on the business, rather than simple usage or reaction metrics!

The Action's Impact

The Track Action is at the very right side of the model because it is the last Action you take before rolling out your learning cluster to the organization despite the fact that you've been considering these measures during the Change and Surround Actions. It's also an ongoing Action that provides feedback and clues to improving the previous four Actions over time, as indicated by the feedback arrow in the model graphic.

Many organizations do not track results, relying instead on intuition, gut feelings, and historical procedures as they design their training programs. Other organizations track Level 1 to determine if learners like a training, based on the idea that if they like it, they are more likely to be learning from it. Others use Level 2 evaluations to prove that participants learned something. But what is the value to the company if participants like it, learn from it, and yet don't do it? L&D can do better. We can prove to ourselves and others that our training drives behavior that drives results. And what if it doesn't? Well, that's learning, too. And who would want to spend their career building things that don't work? Let's dig into the measures, find out what drives behavior and results, and go build those things (Figure 7-2).

Figure 7-2. Summary of Track Action Mindset Shifts

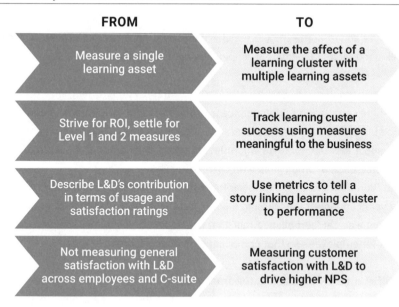

FROM	TO
Measure a single learning asset	Measure the affect of a learning cluster with multiple learning assets
Strive for ROI, settle for Level 1 and 2 measures	Track learning custer success using measures meaningful to the business
Describe L&D's contribution in terms of usage and satisfaction ratings	Use metrics to tell a story linking learning cluster to performance
Not measuring general satisfaction with L&D across employees and C-suite	Measuring customer satisfaction with L&D to drive higher NPS

The Action Implemented

The Track Tool can help you collect your learning from other Actions and convert it into strong measures that demonstrate the impact of L&D's product—the learning cluster. In this section we will walk you through the nuances of the three-step tool (Figure 7-3).

Figure 7-3. Track Tool

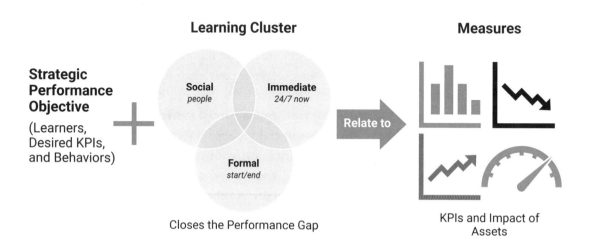

Strategic Performance Objective (Learners, Desired KPIs, and Behaviors)

Learning Cluster — Social *people*, Immediate *24/7 now*, Formal *start/end* — Closes the Performance Gap

Relate to

Measures — KPIs and Impact of Assets

Learning Cluster Name: _____

Learning Cluster Strategic Performance Objective:

Step 1: Select Measures for the Overall Learning Cluster

The purpose of this set of measures is to determine if the approach is working. Can you identify a trend as you build a critical mass of employees who are changing their behavior such that the KPIs improve?

What Is Measured	How to Get Data	Pre-Cluster Value	Goal	Post-Cluster Value
KPI: _____				
Behavior 1				
Behavior 2				

Step 2: Measures for Key Learning Assets

The purpose of this set of measures is to determine if L&D is meeting learner needs and to identify assets whose metrics share a story that gets attention.

Learning Asset	SFI	Metric	Kirkpatrick Level 1–4	Goal	How and When to Get the Data
Example: mentoring program	S	1. % mentees agree mentor helps them perform better 2. testimony from mentees and mentors on their experience	3	1. 70% top 2 box 2. two good stories a quarter	Quarterly 2-question survey of active mentee/mentor pairs (80% response rate)

Step 3: Select a Few Measures to Share

1.
2.
3.
4.
5.

There are three main steps for the Track Tool. The first is to consider how to measure the learning cluster by reviewing the strategic performance objective developed in the Change Action. The second is to identify different methods and metrics for key learning assets, in part by thinking through differences in learning touchpoints. Finally, make strategic choices to narrow down the measures and metrics, and from this reduced list of measures, select a handful that the L&D team would like to report to leadership for this learning cluster.

Step1: Review the Strategic Performance Objective

Identify what is most important to measure for the learning cluster by reviewing your strategic performance objective. If you did a thorough job on the Change Action, you will see that the KPI and behaviors portions outline "what to measure" for the performance of the overall learning cluster. Identify measures of the behavior change that stakeholders expected. Then determine how to get these data. You will likely need to partner with other organizations to get them. Such behavior change measures may be a valuable early predictor that the KPI is about to improve.

Step 2: Review Each Learning Asset

What learning touchpoints do the learning assets fall under? List ways you can get Level 1 Reaction evaluations for each learning asset, with a focus on gathering feedback for asset improvement. Here are some ideas:

- **Videos:** Include a thumbs-up/thumbs-down feature with a comment box. Precede a comment box with a question, such as "Was this helpful?"
- **Job Aids:** On interactive PDF links, include a "Was this helpful? yes/no" question with an open box for inputting "Why or why not?"
- **Peer Coaching or Mentoring:** Have a quick two- or three-question evaluation sheet each party fills out at the end of an interaction. For virtual meetings, this could be a part of a mobile app or online social community tool such as Microsoft Teams.
- **Any Asset:** Measure NPS by simply asking, "Would you recommend this learning asset to others?"

Then go beyond Level 1 by thinking about how learners can demonstrate growth in performance for the learning assets. For Social methods, one way is to let others—perhaps it's the SME or a peer of the learner, or the manager—remark on the growth in performance. Think of ways to capture such remarks within your context. For assets in the immediate learning touchpoint, consider such things as self-evaluation or self-reflection on performance using an L&D-provided rubric. For formal learning touchpoints, try using face-to-face demonstrations of competence.

Consistent qualitative data are important in demonstrating Level 3 Behavior and Level 4 Results. For example, if a learning cluster is on a culture change, and a learning asset is a discussion forum, you could create a weekly word cloud of the forum responses to see the nature of the language changes over time. Imagine how much more powerful these data would be to stakeholders in comparison with simply reporting the number of posts in the forum. This is where emerging technology like big data can really help. (See the Future Technology sidebar to learn more.)

Step 3: Make a Selection

Finally, look through all the methods and metrics you've planned to track. Which ones do you think are most likely to communicate with stakeholders and demonstrate the impact of L&D's work toward the goals of the strategic performance objective? Remember, people pay attention to what you share. Here, you really want to create a separation between metrics that are important for you in L&D, and those that are important for sharing with stakeholders and employees in order to gain sponsorship and awareness of your contributions to their success.

Level 1 evaluation metrics typically become a part of L&D's ongoing improvement strategy, but this type of measure does not necessarily add value for stakeholders and employees. Be careful that you do not expend all your resources responding to Level 1 suggestions for improvements. Instead, step back and look at the bigger picture, selecting Level 3 and 4 evaluation metrics that demonstrate to stakeholders and employees the impact and value of L&D. In your reports and scorecards, always include a measure on the impact of the learning cluster.

The Track Tool represents our current approach to measuring the impact of learning clusters. It's a framework to get you thinking about how different learning assets could require different measures, and how to look at the combined impact of multiple assets on performance change. We encourage you to dig deeper into the topic of measurement, possibly by exploring other proven processes to identify metrics such as:

- **Phillips' ROI Methodology**, which is used by more than 5,000 organizations around the world, systemizes and expands on Kirkpatrick's Levels of Evaluation work. The basis of the methodology is to collect data for a single learning asset at each level of evaluation: efficiency/cost, reaction, learning, application, impact, and ROI (where ROI is strictly a monetary value).
- **Basarab's Predictive Evaluation model**, which centers on identifying the intended goals of a learning asset and the behaviors that need to be adopted by learners. Then, the L&D team strives to predict the percent of learners who will buy into the intended goal and behaviors, thereby creating the ability to calculate the impact on the business.

As the L&D industry moves forward, we need to identify ways to modify these rigorous methods to measure the combined effects of multiple learning assets. If you know of a measurement method, or have ideas to share, please reach out and let us know! Sharing among our own L&D networks is a great way for all of us to continue to build respect for our profession. Then, check back on LearningClusterDesign.com to see which ideas are gaining traction in our industry.

Future Technology–Big Data and L&D

Big data is big news. And now, more than ever, it's available for L&D to use if we learn how.

Volume of Data

Data are everywhere: sales, marketing, operations, research, LMS, internal websites, and more. If your SPO connects to something significant for the business (as it should!), there are probably already metrics being tracked as a part of the business strategy. Reflect on KPIs in your strategic performance objective and find out who is tracking it, and how the data are being tracked. Suggestion: Explore possibilities with IT, who typically knows where the data are. Tap into your customer's data source or look to other organizations in your company.

Data Tools

Data science, machine learning, and deep learning (a subset of machine learning in artificial intelligence) offer some powerful tools that help businesses dive into their data. These tools help uncover patterns and future trends that, if capitalized upon, can maximize the bottom line. Look for historical patterns and use them to help predict future needs of learners and the business through the process of extrapolation.

L&D Capability

What do you need to learn to make big data work for you? Here are some skills that can help:

- **Data strategy skills.** Make sure you are asking the right question, because the question determines the answer you will get! Also, determine the most efficient, accurate way to obtain the data.
- **Data visualization skills.** When you have a lot of data, creating a meaningful presentation can be complex, but visuals can simplify complexity.
- **Critical thinking skills.** Become adept at questioning validity and any biases in the data set or in the interpretations.
- **Technology platform skills.** Seek certificates or training in data visualization systems such as Tableau, xAPI, SAS, other software that is commonly used at your organization.

These are just some of the aspects of big data that may help you understand employee needs, culture trends, and emerging business issues. L&D can get ahead of the requests for more training by using data to strategically choose what learning to build and what infrastructure to develop to support talent development. A word of caution: Big data may set an expectation of needing all the data before moving forward. But that's not how it works. Use what you have, and then extrapolate. It's also important not to use the numbers without thinking. Communicate the full story by sharing not only your data, but your interpretation of it, and your process for forming conclusions. Share your stories and your data with others to gain alternative interpretations and concepts. Then use the data to gain support and move forward with your recommendations.

Keep watch on this area of big data, and if you spot a chance to build your big data muscles, take it!

In Practice

After discovering learning cluster design through our two-day workshop, Sravani Tammiraju at Visa developed and implemented a learning cluster for new hire onboarding. For the Track Action, she decided to tell the story of transformative results in several unique ways. Out of all the measures and metrics she could have reported, she focused on three things: Net Promoter Score, qualitative data, and demonstrated competency through a capstone project. The first time she piloted her learning cluster, the learning cluster received an outstanding NPS of 53. For perspective, an NPS rating above 0 is good, above 50 is excellent, and above 70 is world class.

She gathered a round of feedback and made some changes. After the second implementation, the learning cluster received a best-in-class Net Promoter Score of 87! NPS doesn't just represent a number for her. She knows the learning cluster is demonstrating the value of L&D to employees across the company because, as she relates, "We have people who have been working for two years asking if they can register for this new hire program. It's all spread through word of mouth."

In addition to the power of NPS, she is tracking changes in performance transformation through a promotional video. It provided a way to market the L&D program and the company while creating excitement, buy-in from senior leadership, and global adoption: "One of the things that we did that we've never ever done before was to have someone recording the students as they went through the week. We then consolidated that into a quick two-minute video at the end of the week. We sent the video to senior leaders, who were very pleased with the learning experience early career professionals were going through." This video approach did several things. It provided participants with a resource for spaced learning after the onboarding program, and it shared with leaders and others the value of the learning experience in a very impactful way. As a bonus, this video is now used in recruiting efforts so candidates can see the learning opportunities new hires receive in their first few months of onboarding.

Sravani's new hire program has demonstrated competency development, especially on the technical side. As part of the new hire learning cluster, the learners develop innovative solutions to a current list of challenges in the payments industry, challenges raised by Visa's vice presidents and senior vice presidents. At present, one such idea by a group of six early career professionals has led to a patent application filing through the innovations team at Visa. This learning cluster has been a game changer for Visa and for these hires in the first three months in their career! Visa's leaders are convinced of the power of the learning cluster. According to Sravani, "The response [from leadership] has been phenomenal. The collaboration between leaders and the learning organization has been phenomenal."

By completing the fifth and final Action, Track Transformation of Everyone's Results, Sravani was able to tell the story of what she contributed to the company as an L&D professional. In doing so, she gained further sponsorship, raised awareness of L&D's success throughout the organization, and exceeded expectations for behavior change on the job for new hires. When the story is that powerful, and that convincing, budgetary needs become a forgone conclusion.

Final Note

In this chapter, we shared the new possibilities for evaluating your work based on the new job of taking responsibility for behavior change in the workplace, not just meeting the end-of-class objectives. As the L&D industry shifts into developing and delivering learning clusters, we can be confident of our impact back on the job and on business KPIs and ROI. We talked about how to address the unique challenges of measuring the impact of multiple learning assets and how each learning touchpoint calls for different methods and metrics of measurement. We walked through the tool to help guide your work in this Track Action. To support you further, consider using some of the learning assets listed here to supplement or reinforce what you have gained from this chapter:

- The Track Tool. We've included the most recent version for you in the appendix. For future evolutions, head to LearningClusterDesign.com/Book-Bonus.
- The OK-LCD Learning Cluster (see chapter 9) that we designed to help you grow your capability to use the model in your workplace.
- The chapter 8 example of the OK-LCD model with the five Actions and associated Tools in practice.
- The chapters on the other Actions in the OK-LCD model, so that you can see how each Action supports the others.

Ultimately, this fifth and final Action puts your focus on owning the story stakeholders and employees will hear about successful learning, performance improvement, and your contribution to everyone's results. Because of the core principles of multiple assets and targeting behavior change on the job, the OK-LCD model opens new doors for L&D to gain sponsorship, meaningful insights, and perception as an essential culture-builder in the organization. Rather than focusing only on attendance, usage, and satisfaction, the tool in this final Action encourages you to tell a fuller, more accurate picture of the power of your learning clusters.

Reflect

◊ Does your organization measure the impact of learning initiatives today? How do your current measures compare with those described in this chapter?

◊ What one or two ideas from this chapter empower you to put into practice the Track Transformation for Everyone's Results Action?

◊ How can you shape the story of L&D's work results and contributions differently, or better, than you are doing today?

◊ How can the OK-LCD model make a difference in the following areas for our story characters:
- crafting L&D goals that are meaningful to leadership
- eliminating questions about L&D's worth, impact, and necessity
- moving L&D from an order taker to a competitive advantage for the company?

Apply

◊ Consider the latest learning initiative you are working on. Brainstorm some measures that most likely:
- Demonstrate performance change in the workplace.
- Help you learn about stories that demonstrate the learning cluster success in the workplace.

◊ Look at the Track Tool in the appendix or download a copy from LearningClusterDesign.com /Book-Bonus. Fill out each section to gain deeper practice with the Track Action.

8

Putting It All Together: An OK-LCD Example

"The whole is greater than the sum of its parts."
—Aristotle

In this chapter, we'll look at the OK-LCD model through a fictionalized case study for the GottaLearn Corporation. As you read the GottaLearn case, consider the following:

- How do the five Actions and tools help solve the business challenge?
- What are the benefits of using the OK-LCD model?
- How similar is this case to situations you face? What adjustments would you make for your unique situations?

GottaLearn Corporation and the On-Time-Delivery Performance Gap

Overview: At GottaLearn Corporation, several major projects missed their target completion dates. A study pinpointed the issue: Team members lack time management skills, which led to overpromising deliverables. The L&D team has been asked to "fix" the problem by providing a class on time management for roughly 900 project team members throughout GottaLearn. This time management training is the first major project that will use the OK-LCD model.

Change On-the-Job Behavior Action

The first task is to set the goal for the project using the Change Action. The GottaLearn team analyzed the situation, wrote the strategic performance objective (SPO), and got leadership buy-in to ensure everyone was on the same page.

Writing the SPO

The L&D team read the HR problem-analysis report and discussed what the project sponsor had told them about the situation. To write the SPO, they gathered additional insights through interviews with four groups: team members, project managers, leaders who sign off on project milestones and approve funding, and customer-relations leaders. They spoke with people from projects that had been delivered on time, and from projects that significantly missed their deadlines. The interviews led to some new insights:

- **Team Members.** There are two types of team members: core team members who work on these teams full time, and part-time members who sit on multiple teams and have additional responsibilities outside the team. These part-time members are from functions such as sales, safety, and HR.
- **Technology.** The teams use a cloud-based project management system for tracking tasks, resources, budget, and timelines. The system includes a feature called the Time Management App (TM-App) that can be integrated with an employee calendar to help people stay on track. Only a few projects use the TM-App, and all of those teams met the project deadlines.
- **Existing Time Management Class.** L&D discovered an existing time management classroom course in the LMS. The class was designed for a maximum of 30 people and was typically only half full. The class was run annually and had Level 1 evaluation scores that just barely met L&D standards.

Based on the analysis, the team wrote the strategic performance objective (Figure 8-1).

Figure 8-1. Time Management Strategic Performance Objective (Excerpt From the Change Tool)

By improving *time management skills* for *team members* on projects, the business will benefit from increased customer satisfaction, achieved by *delivering most projects on time, and providing ample warning to management for projects that are off track on schedule.* The changes to on-the-job behavior that we will see among team members include:

- more discussion on what is needed to accomplish tasks in a required timeframe
- increased use of the language related to the time management skills model
- increased user activity on the time management app (TM-App)
- individuals checking their TM-App before committing to due dates
- more frequent conversations about potential risks to project schedules
- more discussions on project barriers that leadership can help overcome.

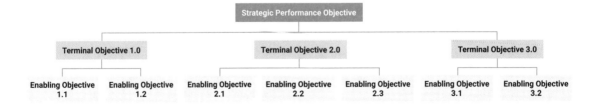

Near Misses

The L&D team almost got off track on the OK-LCD model with two near misses. First, they almost short-cut the process. Their early reaction was to do what they normally would have done: Fix the existing training, make the class mandatory, and deploy it across the company over a few months' time. The L&D team quickly realized they were doing their normal thing and switched gears. They joked about how normally they'd have wrapped up the project with a report on three things: attendance numbers, scores on knowledge checks, and feedback sheets. It was sobering to realize that such a report would indicate that they'd done what was asked but would not have demonstrated L&D's value to the company.

Second, they mistakenly assigned only one asset per skill set. At first, the L&D team contemplated splitting the work into two sets: time management skills and the TM-App. But they quickly realized they were falling into the trap of designing a single learning asset for each skill. Further, their ultimate goal for this project was not to teach skills; their goal was to deliver the business goal of timely project delivery by helping employees close performance gaps. While at first this seemed like a subtle difference, the team realized that this broader goal would cause them to formulate a different solution. The solution would need to be integrated into employees' learning experience and work. The learning cluster format enabled them to do that.

Getting Buy-In Before Proceeding

The learning design team shared the strategic performance objective with the GottaLearn leadership team. At first, the leaders were surprised—hadn't they already told the training team what the objective was? They wanted a training course on time management. But after hearing about the process, here were a few of the reactions from leaders:

- "I'm impressed by the rigor."
- "I feel like you have a clear, accurate idea of what's needed to address the business problem."
- "I can really see the linkage between employee performance and business results—it's not just about teaching a class on time management!"

The leaders provided the team with access to KPI data. This included historic data for on-time delivery, and being placed on the distribution list for KPI data going forward. With these data, the L&D team would be able to see for themselves if their learning cluster was making a difference for the business after it was launched.

Learn Learner-to-Learner Differences Action

The L&D team needed to learn about the differences within their larger target learner group of team members. They wanted to identify groups, or personas, who have the biggest skills gaps with time management, and who might have the largest impact on on-time project delivery. To uncover these differences, the L&D team followed the five steps of the Learn Tool for developing learner personas:

1. Summarize what you already know.
2. Dig deeper into learner differences.
3. Analyze to create learner personas.
4. Create learner persona stories.
5. Use the personas to guide learning asset selection and design.

Step 1: Summarize What You Already Know

The L&D team spent time individually reflecting on who they thought had the most time management trouble and why. They thought about the day-to-day lives of their learners and what kinds of differences they observed between employees. They posted their thoughts in a summary form on SharePoint. Then team members compared notes and filled out the learner persona chart. It was a good start, but there were lots of holes in their chart.

Step 2: Dig Deeper Into Learner Differences

The L&D team sought solid data to help them understand their target learner group. They reviewed three years of data on late-delivery projects to determine the primary trouble spots and read the backward-looking analysis of who or what caused the delays. They interviewed a diverse set of team members, project managers, and some supervisors—different people than those interviewed for the Change Action. They set up an interview protocol to help uncover holes in their learner persona chart, and an online survey helped them gather data from a broader set of target learners. Finally, they used the Learn Tool to help them choose questions for the surveys.

Step 3: Analyze to Create Learner Personas

To develop personas, the L&D team used "The Art of Knowledge Analysis for Creating Learning Personas" from the Learn Tool. It was a creative process that drove a rich understanding of their learner group. At one point in their session, they had 15 different personas! This was a problem. They dug through the data to ferret out which personas would have the biggest impact on the business goal: Deliver on-time projects. That got them down to a reasonable number of personas. An excerpt of the final learner personas is shown in Figure 8-2.

Figure 8-2. Learner Persona Chart (an Excerpt)

Persona Name Short Summary Description	1. Lax Sam A "core" team member who agrees to everything without taking time to realize that he's overbooked.	2. Multitasked Marta A "need-to-know" team member, assigned to review multiple projects, often pulled from one project for high priorities on other projects.	3. Newbie Nasir A team member who is too new to realize what it takes to get something done in the workplace.
Likely Impact on SPO (high, medium, low)	High	Medium	High
1. Key Demographic Differences			
Function	R&D, IT, or other	IT, HR, Health & Safety, Logistics, Finance, and Accounting	All functions
Level	Individual contributor (Level 1 to 2)	Level 2 or 3	New Hire
Tenure	3–8 years	4–15 years	0–2 years
2. Key Learning Need Differences			
Typical Response to Training and Learning	"Sure! I'd be happy to take that course!" He registers but is often a no-show because he's busy executing on his one or two projects.	"Can't go to classes; I have too much to do. I'll have to learn on the job. Send me an e-learning course and I'll run through it."	Learning is a top priority. "Whatever my boss says, I'll do." Has five-plus hours of training per week as part of new hire two-year training program. Wants to learn and do well.
Primary Technology Used	Uses shared sites and documents to deliver work. Can access only from office. Text versus email.	Each function has their own system to use as it relates to project work and approvals. Individuals use email and shared sites most often to do the work. Sends recommendations as email attachments.	Scattered. Uses whatever is handy or mirrors his team members and office mates. Text and IM preferred.
NOTE: No one seems to be using the TM-App. Most are not even aware it exists!			
Preferred Learning Go-Tos	Talk to someone, attend a class. Appreciates reminders.	Search online. Quick e-learning. Recorded webinars. Content must be relevant to what she needs in the moment for her to take the time.	Various. Whatever is recommended or is being used by teammates. More engaged by chunked learning.
Attitude at Work	Harmony, please others, be welcomed onto team.	Get it done; check it off; be respected for personal achievement.	If my manager says "Do it," I'll do it and do it well. I will prove myself and be promoted ASAP.

Figure 8-2. Learner Persona Chart (an Excerpt) *(continued)*

	1. Lax Sam	2. Multitasked Marta	3. Newbie Nasir
3. Key Life-at-Work Differences			
Work Hours	Standard: 8 a.m. to 5 p.m.; with on-site weekend overtime to catch up on critical work	Early: 7 a.m. to 4 p.m.; some evening hours at home for emails and reviewing reports	8 a.m. to 6 p.m.; then off to sports or social gatherings.
Level of Discretionary Time	Mid-high discretion, driven by project meetings	Low; driven by project due dates	Some; guided by manager, has time-bound new hire requirements.
4. Key Performance Gap Differences			
Current Skill/ Performance Level	Poor. Needs to track commitments and realize what commitment entails. Needs to organize calendar to reduce inefficiencies.	Good. Needs to break work into smaller bites and say no or engage manager.	Low. Doesn't know what time or resources are needed to complete tasks but has been thrown into a major project role.
5. Moments of Learning Need (indicate if each moment is likely for each persona Yes/No)			
Learn First Time	Yes; formal setting w/peers	No; just needs reminders	Yes; formal setting
Applying What Was Learned	Yes; tools used in project meetings, reminders by PM	No; already doing it	Yes; tools used in project meetings, reminders by mgr.
When Things Go Wrong	Peer assist, TM SME coach, regular PM check-ins	regular PM check-ins	Mgr. assist, TM SME coach, regular PM check-ins

Step 4: Create Learner Persona Stories

Crafting short summary stories based on the learner personas was fun, creative work. The hardest part was to keep them short and focused on just the critical learner-to-learner differences that would drive learning asset selection later in the project. The end product is shown in Figure 8-3. They had to remind themselves that these are not real people, but they do represent a large segment of the target learner group for this project. They also realized that this set of personas would not be as useful on other projects because it was focused on the time management skill gap, as it should be.

Figure 8-3. Learner Persona Stories

Lax Sam is an individual contributor with a few years of experience. He is a full-time "core" team member tasked with immersive, execution-type tasks for one or two projects at a time. His biggest challenges to time management are that he uses his time inefficiently because he doesn't use systems like the TM-App to help manage his time or estimate the scope and duration of tasks. For this topic, he would like to learn alongside other people and have reminders in the moment.	**Multitasked Marta** is a more senior-level employee handling multiple projects at a time. Her biggest TM challenges are 1) getting timely inputs from "core" team members and 2) being required to spend unplanned volumes of time on higher-priority issues for other projects. She needs to involve her project managers and boss more quickly to address above issues earlier than she does now. For this topic, she would like to learn on the go.	**Newbie Nasir** is a recent college graduate who is trying to prove himself and so wants to learn how to do time management right from the beginning. His primary job is learning, but his biggest challenges for time management are that he has no previous experience or context for what commitments require in the real world, and he doesn't know where the right people or resources are to include when needed. For this topic, he would like to learn deep, fast, and in social environments, so that he can then get to application quickly.

Step 5: Using Personas to Brainstorm Learning Assets

With the learner personas still fresh in their heads, the L&D team filled out the last section of the Learn Tool—ideas for learning assets that this persona might appreciate. An excerpt of their work is shown in Figure 8-4. This would give them a head start when they got to the Surround Action.

Figure 8-4. Table of Ideas for Learning Assets

Ideas for Learning Assets That This Persona Might Appreciate		
Persona Name	1. Lax Sam • Classes • Lunch & learns • "Learning moments" as push notifications from the app	2. Multitasked Marta • E-learning • Time management page of links • Test-out opportunities • Coaching from project leader	3. Newbie Nasir • Case study blogs "When things go wrong vs. right" • Classes • Time management page of links • Peer or mentor coaching

Adjusting and Confirming

The L&D team selectively shared these personas with a few insiders in the field—project managers, supervisors, and the like—to confirm their validity. They made a few adjustments. As they reflected on their work so far, they realized it was different from their normal ADDIE Analyze work for a target audience. The five parts of the Learn Tool guided them to collect information about the learners that was more closely linked to the business issue of delivering projects on time, instead of just the time management skill gap. Not to mention that they now would be meeting the needs of three separate learner personas, rather than one target audience. The L&D team was confident that this would influence the final L&D product so that it would deliver the business KPIs and desired on-the-job behaviors, to the benefit of all.

Upgrade Existing Assets Action

The L&D team realized that the existing time management class provided an opportunity for a quick start toward a solution. But that course needed modernization!

A Working Meeting

The L&D team set up a working meeting to determine how to upgrade the existing two-day time management class. Their meeting agenda was based on the Upgrade Tool.

Time Management Class Upgrade Agenda
- Refresher on SPO and learner personas
- Review of existing time management class (materials, content, ratings)
- Apply the Upgrade Action 3 Tool process:
  - Step 1: Rate the existing asset. Does it have each of the nine elements of modernness?
  - Step 2: Is it possible to include this element? Yes/No.
  - Step 3: If unlimited by reality, list ideas to include or improve on this element.
  - Step 4: Are the ideas feasible now or later?
  - Step 5: Based on what you are willing to do now, name the modernized asset and assign a new rating to confirm it is more modern.
- Next steps

A snapshot of their results at different stages of the process is shown in Figures 8-5, 8-6, and 8-7.

Figure 8-5. Excerpt of Step 1 and 2 Upgrade Tool for Time Management Skills

Existing Asset Name: Two-day class. One a year. 30 ppl/class.	Step 1 Rate Current (1=Y; 0=N)	Step 2 Possible? (Y/N)
Elements of Modernness		
Accessible	0	y
Autonomous	0	y
Chunked	0	y
Current	1	y
Experiential	1	y
For Me	0	y
Hyperlinked	0	y
MVAK	1	y
Social	1	y
Modernness Rating	4	

Figure 8-6. Upgrade Tool Step 3: Brainstorming Improvements by Element

Accessibility

- Add a **TM landing page** that will link to class registration and all other TM learning assets.
- Repurpose class content as how-to **job aids** for the app.
- Crowdsource "Real Life Situations" **case studies**. (Especially for Marta!)
- Could learners **live chat** with experienced PMs about questions about scope or commitment?

Autonomous

- **E-learning** (not in budget, takes time to produce).
- To-do app already exists; is there a way to **leverage notifications** to provide learning? IT says yes! (Especially for Sam and Marta.)

Chunked

- Convert existing f2f class to **chunked virtual** using web conf technology.
- Homework: Summarize and share learning content (crowdsourcing for **future job aids**).

Current

- Keep training current on software updates for PM system and TM app. (Consider a **new IT tool** for performance support.)
- Add new **"Real Life" case studies** to make it feel current.
- Future: L&D staff could run **book clubs** on TM topics annually.

Experiential

- Design an **interaction** every 2-4 min, as well as activities, reflections, and shared learning as homework.

For Me

- Learners can choose what **job aids** they need based on good tagging.
- **Share virtual class topics** in advance and provide **knowledge checks** to test out. (Especially for Marta.)
- Don't require via LMS? Instead add reco/NPS from peers.

Hyperlinked

- Anything TM training-wise gets linked to LMS **TM landing page**.
- Include **resource links in the virtual class** as well as in the app's **push notifications**.

MVAK

- Future: Virtual class could **create videos**.
- IT suggests **gamifying the app**—the app has a leaderboard feature that tracks logins that's currently inactive but could be leveraged. (Especially for Nasir.)

Social

- Based on initial demand, run several **classroom** cohorts.
- Homework to connect with another **cohort** member about the TM topic. (Especially for Nasir and Sam.)

Figure 8-7. Upgrade Tool Steps 4 and 5: Select Upgrade Plan and Re-Rate Modernness Score

Existing Asset Name: Two-day class. One a year. 30 ppl/class.	Step 1 Rate Current (1=Y; 0=N)	Step 3 Summarized Ideas for Element	Step 4 Now or Later? (N/L)	Step 5 Rating for Upgrade Plan: Virtual ILT Class and Job Aids Housed on TM Landing Page in LMS Notifications and Game on TM App
Elements of Modernness				
Accessible	0	• TM landing page • How-to job aids • Real life case studies • Live chat feature	N N L L	1
Autonomous	0	• E-learning • TM app notifications	L N	1
Chunked	0	• 1 hr/wk virtual class • Job aid	N L	1
Current	1	• IT tool for software updates • Real life case studies • Book clubs	N L L	1
Experiential	1	• Virtual class interactions	N	1
For Me	0	• Share topics in advance • Test out knowledge checks	N N	0
Hyperlinked	0	• TM landing page has all links • Resource links in all content	N N	1
MVAK	1	Videos Leaderboard on TM app	L N	1
Social	1	1 hour/week virtual class New cohort each month	N	1
Modernness Rating	**4**			**8**

The CLO Review

The L&D team needed the CLO's buy-in for the new time management course design so they could quickly get the resources for production. They shared their work and made the following points:

- This represents some modernization without going overboard.
- The solution is feasible, given timeframe and the resources needed.
- The solution is in line with the strategic performance objective (Change Action).
- The solution is in line with the learner personas (Learn Action).
- Here are our assumptions about what we can do now versus later. (Do you agree?)

- Request: resources and people to execute the solution (IT, SMEs, TM-App owner, L&D design group, and L&D delivery group).

The CLO noted the following strengths in their proposed upgrade:

- improved learner retention by chunking webcast courses
- reduced L&D workload by repurposing existing content for how-to job aids
- improved employee access to time management training by using ILT virtual class
- stronger L&D relationship with IT by partnering on the landing page and TM-App features
- improved speed of access to resources with a time management landing page on the LMS
- future possibilities to be deployed later, such as live chat, e-learning, and real-life case studies
- infrastructure ideas to support learning assets for the Surround Action, including blog software, "Best Job Aid" contest platform, webpage for recommended books with reader and leader comments, video-sharing software.

Best of all, the L&D team's upgrade plan could be accomplished in just a few weeks. That left sufficient time and resources for the Surround Action and learning cluster design.

Surround Learners With Meaningful Learning Assets Action

The GottaLearn L&D team designed the Time Management Learning Cluster across two meetings. In the first meeting they completed steps 1-4 from the Surround Tool. In a second meeting, they accomplished step 5—assign terminal and enabling objectives for each learning asset in the learning cluster.

Steps 1-3 were easy—a summary of the previous three Actions. But the summary reminded the L&D team to continue building on what they had already done, rather than design in isolation on the time management topic.

There are four parts to step 4: brainstorm, converge, map assets to the three learning touchpoints, and final checks.

Brainstorm

The L&D team did a brainstorming exercise. They wrote ideas for learning assets on sticky notes. They warmed up by taking the ideas generated during the Learn and Upgrade Actions and making them more specific.

For example, Multitasking Marta's need for e-learning became three sticky notes: e-learning on GottaLearn's time management model, e-learning on TM-App from the software supplier, and a "what to do when you are in a pinch" e-learning challenge on how to spot when you are in trouble and how to seek help (using video scenarios).

They used a different color sticky note for each persona. Some sticky notes were duplicated in two or three colors. That's a good thing: Meeting multiple persona needs with one learning asset.

Converge

With a room full of sticky notes, they grouped the notes by color and persona. Then they asked the writer of these notes to clarify their thoughts for each possible learning asset. Duplicate ideas were eliminated. Similar ideas were merged. Ideas that showed up for all three personas were rewritten on a fourth-color sticky note.

Next, they discussed which ideas were not feasible in the short run. These were not eliminated, just put off to the side for possible consideration later in the project or for another time altogether.

Map Assets to the Three Learning Touchpoints

For this next activity, they could have done the mapping exercise by continuing to use the sticky notes, as they had done in their training session on the OK-LCD model. They chose a different method. To give them a jump start on documenting their work, they moved to a virtual sticky notes environment using an online whiteboard software.

In this virtual environment, the learning touchpoints Venn diagram was on the whiteboard. The L&D team moved the virtual sticky notes to appropriate locations on the Venn diagram to indicate the degree to which each asset reached the persona in the social, immediate, or formal space.

The sticky-note placement choices drove helpful discussion. For example, the time management class and e-learning courses were originally placed at the bottom of the "formal" circle. Their discussion led them to realize the need to move live classes toward "social" to acknowledge the personal interaction that happens in this environment. This type of interaction is something that Lax Sam seeks out in his learning choices. The e-learning was moved closer to the "immediate" circle to acknowledge that e-learning tended to be an anytime, anywhere asset. This is just what Multitasking Marta needed. But the team noted that some e-learning might be strictly "formal" if it required management sign-off before it could be accessed. This was typical of external e-learning programs, when sign-off was needed for budget-control reasons.

After the L&D team had agreed on placement of all the assets, they took a step back and reviewed their work. They quickly realized that they were missing a few learning touchpoints for specific personas. They added the following:

- For Newbie Nasir: An experienced-mentor program to help build an internal network and aid in understanding of the time commitment needed for tasks (social and formal touchpoint).
- For Lax Sam: A book club for discussing real-life issues with others (social touchpoint).
- For Multitasking Marta: A project leader peer-coaching option (social touchpoint), as well as an online job aid page with a question and comment section (social and immediate touchpoints).

The resulting learning cluster is shown in Figure 8-8.

Figure 8-8. Excerpt of Time Management Learning Cluster

Lax Sam	White
Newbie Nasir	Light gray
Multi-tasker Marta	Dark gray
All Personas	Black

Time Management Learning Assets	Description/Comments
Virtual classroom	20 sessions for core TM concepts, over six weeks, by cohort
Self-assessment	Randomized question set, one for core TM concept
TM wiki	Using existing shared-file program, post navigable/indexed one-page info sheets organized by core concepts and tiered enabling objectives. Titles are searchable. Learners can add content, "likes," and comments to help learners and L&D identify best content.

Note: All assets cover time management, unless otherwise specified. See learning objectives for details.

Check and Recheck

Having completed the learning cluster graphic, the team stood back and took a moment to admire their very first learning cluster design. Then they ran through the checklist questions.

Q: Do you have a learning asset for each learning touchpoint for each persona?
A: Yes, now that we have added a few more for each persona.

Q: Are there any needs uncovered from your learner personas that are not being met?
A: Newbie Nasir wants to do the e-learning course at home, but access is unavailable.

Q: Do the learning assets further the strategic performance objective (SPO)?
A: Yes. Each learning asset is focused on changing behavior on the job for improved TM skills and ability to deliver on time. See learning objectives and design for details.

Step 5. Assign Terminal and Enabling Objectives to Each Learning Asset

At the step 5 meeting, the L&D team went to work developing and assigning objectives for each learning asset. While traditional thinking might have jumped to developing objectives for each learning asset independently, this time, with the OK-LCD model, they would view the objectives as a whole across the learning cluster. The team started by reviewing the business goal in the SPO, following the OK-LCD model principle to "design the whole, not just the parts." They considered what the learners needed to achieve the business imperative: Deliver on-time projects, or, at minimum, alert management when a project is off schedule. They proposed a global list of terminal objectives and critical enabling objectives that could be used by multiple assets across the learning cluster. This approach continued to increase their confidence that the learning cluster and each asset would help achieve the expected results.

Then, they began to match the objectives to each learning asset (see a snapshot of the cross-referencing process in Figure 8-9). Not every objective was used by every asset, and some were used by multiple assets. That's because assets were intentionally designed for different personas and different moments of learning need. The team iterated through multiple cycles of reviewing each persona's needs, the objectives, and the learning assets:

- Did Sam (or Martha or Nasir) get all the learning objectives they needed through the learning assets they were most likely to use?
- For their moments of learning need, was there a learning asset that would be readily available?
- Was there sufficient repetition of content for critical objectives within the asset mix to provide spaced learning?

Through the process, they discovered that one or two objectives weren't addressed in a connecting learning asset. This was dealt with by either adding content to an existing asset, or in rare cases, adding a learning asset.

Figure 8-9. Excerpt From Surround Action Step 5

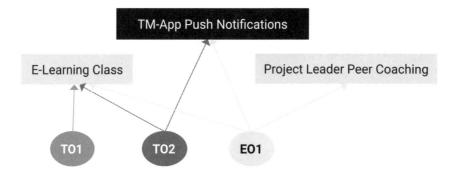

Snapshot of global list of terminal and enabling objectives:

TO1: Describe the GottaLearn Company's time management model

TO2: Demonstrate how the TM-App guides your project plan timing

EO1: Explain the three-step process on the TM-App to alert project manager or leader of schedule delay issues

KEY:
TO = Terminal Objective
EO = Enabling Objective

TM-App Push Notifications

E-Learning Class

Project Leader Peer Coaching

TO1   TO2   EO1

Wrapping Up Design and Development

The learning cluster was designed, but now the individual learning assets needed to be fully designed, developed, and implemented. For each learning asset, an L&D team member took responsibility for this next stage. Thankfully, the CLO had provided additional resources to help them.

Depending on the nature of each learning asset, they used different methods for asset development. For example, they could get off-the-shelf assets, upgrade existing assets, or do a full development using ADDIE, SAM, or other familiar methods. In a few cases, they chose to crowdsource smaller assets, such as job aids, by repurposing the outcomes of activities from the now-upgraded time management virtual ILT class.

Track Transformation of Everyone's Results Action

The GottaLearn L&D team scheduled a Track Action design session to figure out measures for this learning cluster using the three steps in the Track Tool. They needed to move quickly because their choices could affect design. For example, online assets had to be set up to capture certain data, how and where assets were placed in the LMS affected which data features would be turned on, and self-assessment tools needed to be designed to incorporate the measures. And they needed to hurry to grab baseline data before the learning cluster went live. While baseline numbers are typically depressing, the only way to prove improvement is to get current data to compare against in the future.

Step 1: Select Measures for the Overall Learning Cluster

For the measures meeting, the L&D team invited the IT person assigned to the time management project. They explained their need to identify good measures of on-the-job behavior change and the impact of the whole learning cluster, not just one asset.

The IT person showed the L&D team what was possible—things that they had no idea existed that could be delivered as a regular report. This was L&D's first attempt to use Big Data from the LMS. Figure 8-10 shows the data they landed on.

Figure 8-10. Measures for the Overall Learning Cluster

What Is Measured	How to Get Data	Pre-Cluster #	Goal	Post-Cluster #
KPI: % on-time project delivery	Data report approved by sponsor	Need baseline data now!	↑10% 1st yr ↑30% 2nd yr goal: 85% on time	
High integrity—mgrs hear about changes to delivery projections	Quarterly; one-question quiz to mgrs.	Need baseline data now!	10% improved 1st yr 50% better 2nd yr	
Increased use of TM-App associated with calendar	Report by # of users and freq. of use (avg. by user, org., and project)	4% users Avg. freq 7x/day	50% users among target Avg >5/day for 1st year	
Team members give realistic completion dates	Quarterly; one-question quiz to proj. mgrs.	Need baseline data now!	Improvement: • 1st yr: 20% • 2nd yr: 40%	

Step 2: Measures for Key Learning Assets

For individual learning asset measures, the L&D team considered their normal data, mostly usage and satisfaction numbers. They'd keep some of them, like Level 1 evaluations. But some were no longer pertinent in a learning cluster world. For example, how many people attend a class is no longer valid when there were other options for learning, while "percent of available classroom seats filled" was still a valid measure of efficiency. For many learning assets related to social and immediate learning touchpoints, they'd never thought about measuring these, so they were in uncharted waters.

Again, IT helped them understand what data might be available, and how to get current data more easily. It was eye-opening. For example, they learned they could add push notifications to ask learners if they would recommend the TM-App, thereby giving them an NPS measure.

Step 3: Select a Few to Share

The L&D team had gotten carried away with a long list of measures. In reality, they needed just enough to ensure that the cluster and assets were meeting needs. They scaled back by asking themselves:

- How often do we need to collect, interpret, and report these data?
- Who will have time to look at these data and interpret it?
- When we get a result, how will we know if the number or answer is a good thing?

Then they asked, "How will we report the business impact of the time management learning cluster to the GottaLearn C-suite?" While they had included all the metrics and KPIs from the strategic performance objective, they realized that all their data were quantitative. They needed to add qualitative data stories of success to help the numbers come alive. For example, they created a place for testimonials about the mentoring program, and they added a post-class question: "What did you do differently as a result of this class?" The list of measures for learning assets was scaled back, and a few qualitative measures were added. An excerpt of the list is shown in Figure 8-11.

Figure 8-11. Select Measures for Key Learning Assets

Learning Asset	SFI	Metric	Kirkpatrick Level 1–4	Goal	How and When to Get the Data
Virtual class on TM	SF	Smile sheets. Learner prediction of % material they will apply on the job	1 and 2	> 80% Ex/VGd avg > 80% apply	Smile sheet report from LMS
TM-App (Add-on for company calendar software)	I	NPS	1	>50%	Push notification question: Would they recommend the app to a peer?
TM wiki	SI	1st qtr: contributors=15, hits=180, comments=35. Reassess thereafter	2 and 3	3 stories per qtr.	Assign L&D person to review wiki and report numbers and stories
Project leader coaching	S	% of responses rate a 4 or 5 (top 2 box)	3	>80%	Pulse survey, monthly, on confidence that your project schedule reflects reality
Mentoring program	S	• % mentees agree mentor helps them perform better • Testimony from mentees and mentors on their experience	3	• 70% top 2 box • 2 good stories a quarter	Quarterly two-question survey of active mentee/mentor pairs (80% response rate)
Learning cluster	n/a	% on-time project delivery	4	85% on time by year 3	Data report approved by sponsor

They had enough data now to write the reports for the C-suite. They could pull from both quantitative and qualitative measurement data for the learning cluster, and add some individual learning asset measures. With this information, they felt they could capture people's attention with a story about the transformations of everyone's results—the business, the employee, and the L&D organization.

Introduce the Learning Cluster to Stakeholders

To enroll everyone in the learning cluster and future use of the OK-LCD model, the design team hosted a lunch & learn. They invited the leadership, key stakeholders, and others within L&D and HR. The

L&D team summarized each Action's process and outcomes on five individual posters. The posters were placed around the room and an L&D team member was stationed at each one to answer questions.

This lunch was, in reality, a moment of celebration for L&D, as they took this big step toward modernizing their approach to learning design. The CLO kicked it off by welcoming everyone, and then describing the overall design difference. "With the OK-LCD model, our approach and outcome feels different, and better than our usual design process. In the past, when someone asked for a training program, that's what we gave you. Now, we are giving you something new—a learning cluster. It's designed to help employees deliver the on-the-job performance needed to meet our business challenges and achieve our business goals. For our employees, this modern learning design approach provides learning opportunities at just the right places, times, and ways so that they feel more engaged, valued, and confident that they are learning here at GottaLearn."

She unveiled a sixth poster that she herself had created. It provided her perspective on what she saw as the L&D team's achievements as they used the OK-LCD process for the first time (Figure 8-12).

Figure 8-12. What Was Different About This TM Project

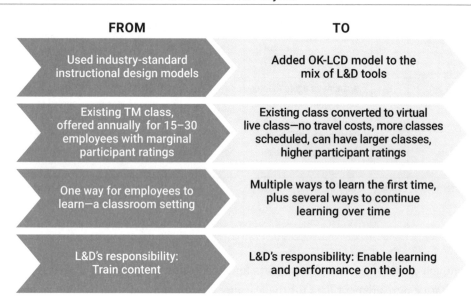

FROM	TO
Used industry-standard instructional design models	Added OK-LCD model to the mix of L&D tools
Existing TM class, offered annually for 15–30 employees with marginal participant ratings	Existing class converted to virtual live class—no travel costs, more classes scheduled, can have larger classes, higher participant ratings
One way for employees to learn—a classroom setting	Multiple ways to learn the first time, plus several ways to continue learning over time
L&D's responsibility: Train content	L&D's responsibility: Enable learning and performance on the job

People walked around the room talking with the team members who were standing by each Action poster. The CMO commented, "This all just makes so much sense. I just want to keep my customers satisfied with on-time project delivery. I thought more classes would do that. But I'm seeing how a class could be so far from where an employee might need to learn. And a class might not be offered at the right time for the employee."

Another leader remarked, "Sometimes learning something formally might not be the only way to help someone do better on the job. They might need a social push or an immediate answer. It's great to see how this new learning cluster approach can provide that for our employees."

The next deliverable to the leadership team would be the progress reports after the learning cluster was launched. This was a good start for a new process to design modern learning at GottaLearn Corporation.

New Considerations for the Future

Now that the team had executed the OK-LCD model for the first time, there were several important points to keep in mind.

The first was to consider existing infrastructure GottaLearn had, but L&D wasn't using. For future learning clusters, they could take advantage more of the tools employees were already using, like the GottaLearn Wiki and the GottaLearn Viewer (equivalent of YouTube). Even the regular company newsletters could have learning tips and reminders.

The second was to think about how resources could be efficiently used. Some of these learning assets can be used as part of the virtual classes and repurposed for use on the job. And, because there is so much material and so few L&D staffers, L&D could get help by having the learners in the classes create some of the one-pagers and videos as part of their class assignments.

The third was to start looking at patterns across the infrastructure L&D continues to use. For example, they were already getting the hang of using push notifications and reminders with the time management app. What other topics could use automated reminders as a part of the learning cluster? For any new technology the team decides to bring in the future, some form of notification will be a requirement.

Lastly, it is important to remember that it wasn't necessary to squeeze everything into just one learning asset. Knowing this can feel like a big burden being lifted from the designer's shoulders. If the learner wasn't ready to learn at the moment, other L&D assets will be in place for the learners' next moments of learning need.

Final Note

Through the GottaLearn case study, you have seen how a team organized and executed the OK-LCD process. You also saw how they communicated the principles and values of the OK-LCD model to the rest of the organization. Finally, you read how they navigated common pitfalls when implementing the model.

Seeing the OK-LCD model from start to finish shows how the simple Actions build to create a powerful, effective result—far different from the norm. Doing it once for one learning challenge is a huge accomplishment. But what if you want to evolve your L&D organization? In the next chapter, we highlight an organization that is doing just that, and we talk about issues to keep in mind when building a learning cluster–based organization.

Reflect

As you reflect on the GottaLearn Corporation case study and its implications for your own adoption of the OK-LCD model, consider each of the following questions:

◊ How did the use of each of the Actions and Tools help in solving the business challenge?

◊ What were the benefits of using the OK-LCD model?

◊ How similar is this case to situations you face? What adjustments would you make for your unique situations?

◊ Since time management is often viewed as a basic skill, what challenges do you see applying in OK-LCD to a more complex performance gap? How could you overcome these challenges?

Apply

Consider a learning design project you are working on or about to start. Begin to practice designing for modern learning. Create a visually rich poster presentation that shows an excerpt of each of the five Tools, sketched out for your project. We encourage you to use the poster to share your thoughts with others about using the OK-LCD model where you work.

Your Learning Cluster Design Poster:

◊ Title your poster to concisely summarize the problem you are trying to solve (examples: *Frontline Sales Skills, New Hire Onboarding, High-Potential Leadership Development*)

◊ Write out the **strategic performance objective** (terminal and enabling objectives are optional).

◊ Show **learner personas**. We suggest two to four for your first practice of OK-LCD.

◊ **Describe an upgrade** for one existing learning asset, if applicable.

◊ Create a **visual of your learning cluster** using the Venn diagram of social, formal, and immediate learning touchpoints and showing your balance of learning assets across the learner personas.

◊ List measures to **track transformation of everyone's results**. List just a few that tell the story of progress toward the strategic performance objective.

9

Envisioning Your Future
Designing Modern Learning

"One of the great errors organizations make is shutting down what is a natural, life-enhancing process—chaos. We are terrified of chaos. But if you move out of control, you understand that the only way a system changes is when it is far from equilibrium. And you can't reorganize to a higher level unless you risk the perils of the path through chaos."
—Margaret J. Wheatley

odels are "sense-making" tools. In a world that is shifting and changing at an ever-increasing rate, it is comforting to have a new model that can help us make sense of that change. A model gives us confidence and competence as we take new actions and adopt new ways.

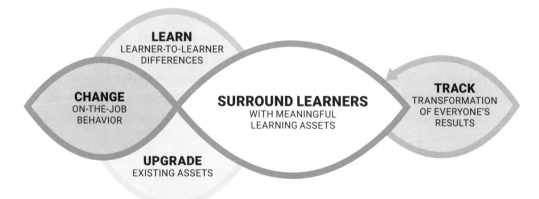

Are you experiencing any of the things in the first column of Figure 9-1? By now, we hope you can see how each of the five Actions can move you to the right-hand column.

Figure 9-1. From Only ADDIE, SAM, and Other ID Models to OK-LCD

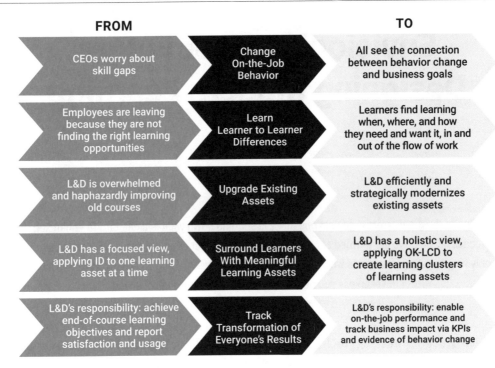

You become a part of the next L&D evolution—beyond ADDIE, SAM, blended learning, Agile, design thinking—as you adopt the OK-LCD model, the philosophy and principles, as well as its Actions and associated Tools. Try it once and see what happens. Then try it again. Scale up, and eventually, every learning initiative will have a learning cluster. This chapter focuses on enabling you to evolve your ID model—and to lead the next evolution for the L&D industry. We'll share the story of a company already living the OK-LCD principles and philosophies. We'll describe common implementation barriers and ways around them. We'll paint a picture of L&D partnering inside and outside, as L&D becomes a central part of the industry network. Finally, we'll focus on building our own L&D skills for the future L&D.

An L&D Organization Already in the Future

"The future is already here. It is just unevenly distributed." —William Gibson

When the world is ripe for an invention, it is frequently discovered in several separate places within a similar timeframe. When we interviewed Comcast's L&D leadership team, we quickly realized that this theory of "simultaneous invention" was at play. Comcast is already living the principles and philosophies embodied in the OK-LCD model. They are even using some of the OK-LCD language! Comcast is a great example of what it looks like when an L&D organization is designing for modern learning.

Background

Comcast is a global media and technology company that employs more than 180,000 people. The L&D organization at Comcast is centralized. This centralized structure provides the benefit of scale for infrastructure purchases and use. And centralization improves efficiency by assigning one individual or team to design each training, rather than several divisions or regions trying to do the same thing with fewer resources. Comcast's L&D organization comprises 500 professionals who are training delivery experts, instructional designers and technologists, and program managers. Here's a look at their approach to designing modern learning, the infrastructure needed to scale the approach, and the results they have gained.

Modern Learning Design Approach Consistent With OK-LCD Principles

Comcast's L&D department aligns themselves strongly with the business. They used the term *learning products* to highlight that these L&D deliverables have inherent value to the business and serve as investments in Comcast employees. The learning organization runs their teams as a business and has "earned their business relationships," says Keith DeAngelis, leader for learning and development, to support Comcast's residential customers. They've also moved beyond a transactional view of L&D. As Martha Soehren (2019), chief talent development officer, stated in *TD* magazine: "Measurement is no longer just about proving the TD function's worth. Rather, it is about enabling the organization—and especially TD leaders—to maximize the value that the TD function provides."

Comcast's learning organization's process for developing learning follows closely with what we've described in this book:

- They begin by asking the business, "What KPI is expected to improve as a result of this work?"
- They develop learner personas.
- They deliver a variety of learning assets, grouped by topic, all accessible through their LMS.
- They track feedback of each asset as well as an evaluation for the grouping—both efficiency metrics and impact metrics, which include both qualitative and quantitative measures.

New Infrastructure to Support a New Philosophy

To achieve their business goals, and do so efficiently and repeatably, Comcast L&D realized they needed their own technology tools beyond an industry-standard LMS. Some of these tools are proprietary. Others have been developed for them by external suppliers and licensed for public sale. Here's a snapshot of some of the new systems Comcast's learning organization built:

- **Single Source of Truth (SST) Platform:** With more than 200 learning initiatives in the works, training delivery experts were struggling to find trainer support materials for their programs. Rather than going through 10 different sources, Comcast created a visually and functionally appealing platform using SharePoint that houses anything a trainer needs and is always guaranteed to be up-to-date.

- **Star Chamber SME teams.** This is a communication structure developed to collect updates from learners, the business, and trainers. Frontline supervisors—the people who see the work every day—serve as SMEs and are incentivized to participate in L&D initiatives through badging and collecting points that can be used to purchase products or make donations to charity. The SMEs' role is to provide feedback and updates to ensure the training is consistent with what is happening in the field. These SMEs review trainers' feedback and new ideas, annotate the training content within the Star Chamber as needed, and even submit videos to the program managers to be used within a training product to augment participant learning.

- **Measuring impact.** Soehren believes strongly in "showing the return to the business one story at a time." She counsels that tracking transactional data, such as cost, participation, and so on, is essential. But it must go beyond that to track impact. One way that Comcast tracks impact is through sharing success stories. Trainers at Comcast are taught to be on the lookout for success stories, which they validate through their business customers before bringing them to the National Executive Learning Council. At these quarterly council sessions, senior leaders from across Comcast's business units dedicate time to sharing success stories. In addition, Comcast's HR team has partnered internally with the business intelligence team to bring meaningful predictive analytics to life. Training the L&D team on the latest in data analysis is a key part of making sure tracking impact is successful.

- **Portal Making Machine (PMM).** Comcast partnered with MakeSense Design Co. to custom build a learning journey portal that brings together informal and formal, self-serve, and planned learning assets. Learners had been skipping prework because it was in a different location than the LMS. Now, with the Portal Making Machine, each learning initiative has a portal in which people in multiple roles are involved, such as the manager, the mentor, approvers, and, of course, the learner. The portals follow an *Awareness—Learn—Practice—Demonstrate* framework. The learner goes through all parts of the framework, and people in the other roles interact with the learner at strategically selected points within the framework. Again, training is a key part of enabling the infrastructure; for example, mentors in the system receive training and a toolkit to support their participation.

When designing modern learning at scale, streamlined systems like these are required to free L&D to focus on making a difference to the business.

Learning Assets That Meet Needs

By marrying a deep understanding of learner needs and the business goals with L&D skills and new technologies, Comcast's L&D produces learning that works. Here are two examples of the impact of Comcast's learning initiatives.

E-learning to augmented reality (AR) conversion. A critical e-learning course needed significant content updates. It was going to be expensive because it was an animated e-learning course. Technicians needed this training to help them better understand how the "signal network to customers" technology works, so the technicians could help maintain signal flow and troubleshoot issues in the field. As part of the training, after completing the animated e-learning course, technicians would take a physical tour of the head-end facility (a hub where signals are transported through the Comcast network to customers). Comcast L&D could have simply updated the existing course, but animation changes are expensive. Instead, they looked at what learners needed and proposed a way to make it even better and more cost-effective! They used a preferred supplier to develop training that was followed by an immersive virtual reality tour of the head-end facility. An additional benefit: The virtual tour reduced physical risks of damage to the head-end equipment and eliminated the need for head-end technicians to take time from their work to conduct in-person tours. The results:

- World-class NPS: 81.7 percent of learners said they would recommend the course, with 83 percent saying they would recommend the delivery approach.
- Saved about 800 employee hours of in-person tours over a one-year period.

90-day onboarding program. Previous studies showed that onboarding program results were better when there was an engaged mentor and supervisor involved. So, a four-week ILT course was replaced by a self-serve portal in which social learning occurred through the engagement of a mentor and a manager, who took on the role of approver. The key was to make it simple and easy for everyone to interact on the portal. The way it works is that each person in a support role receives email notifications that link them directly to the work screen when assignments are complete and ready for review. Evaluations in the system include both quantitative and qualitative components. Approvers can respond by providing feedback in the form of comments, and use quantitative scoring to ensure new hires are hitting the target. Learners fill out questionnaires to evaluate the help received from their mentor and the difference it made. As manager and mentor involvement goes up, so do new hire performance and engagement. Managers who were engaged with the self-serve platform had lower attrition rates in their organizations than those managers who were not.

Comcast follows the principles we've spelled out in this book for designing modern learning: They change employee performance on the job, offer multiple learning assets in and out of the flow of work, and focus on learner needs and situations. The results show a world-class learning organization already living in the future.

Becoming the L&D of the Future

We in L&D know, better than most, how difficult change is for people and organizations. Perhaps you yourself have developed change management training to help others deal with these difficulties. Now it's time for us to apply these change management principles. In doing so, we will become part of the future of L&D.

Envisioning Success

Let's first recall the benefits described by the companies profiled in the "In Practice" features throughout the book (Figure 9-2):

- **Bluescape Software** saw an increase in budget, an increase in training resources, and a new belief that learning assets would have a business impact. They also began discussions for a new L&D-based business product for their company (chapters 2 and 4).
- **Visa Inc.** received best-in-class NPS scores for their onboarding work, through developing a learning cluster that spoke to the "for me" need of modern learners. With strategic use of quantitative and qualitative metrics, L&D clearly demonstrated everyone's results and L&D's contribution to the business (chapters 4 and 7).
- **The Gorilla Glue Company** efficiently met the needs for revamping 78 training topics by delivering learning clusters instead. The fast pace and low cost of this solution was an added bonus. Managers now ask for L&D to apply their learning expertise to help solve problems, rather than to just design training (chapter 6).
- **Paycor** met the business need to increase managerial capability among a diverse set of employees with their Aspiring Managers learning cluster. By considering the needs of each persona, Paycor L&D created a learning cluster that works. Aspiring Managers graduates receive higher engagement from their direct reports, and higher "coaching index" scores than those who have not experienced this learning cluster. And the qualitative data show that the cluster has facilitated breaking through organizational silos, increasing internal networking, and driving ongoing discussion on the core managerial competencies (chapters 5 and 6).

Figure 9-2. Traditional L&D vs. Learning Cluster Design Results

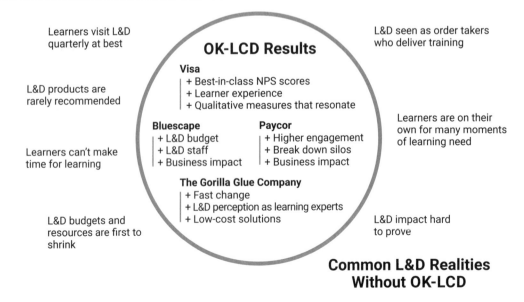

Managing Resistance to Change

Achieving results similar to those described in this book and implementing learning clusters as an organization-wide strategy usually involve navigating some chaos. We recommend that you brush off your best change management model and apply what you know.

As part of change management, identify what will change—either intentionally or inadvertently as a by-product of the chaos. We encourage you to review the many "From/To Shifts" figures throughout the book. These describe what is changing. You will need to consider who is affected by these changes and work with them to make the shift successfully.

In our work with others, the typical chaos includes organizational culture, budget, L&D staffing, and L&D staff capability. Here is a summary of advice from us and others in our network.

Organizational Culture

The existing perception of L&D, L&D's job, and L&D's success metrics can often be the biggest barrier to getting started. We want to change stakeholders, customers, and learners' expectations of what L&D offers, from training programs to learning clusters. Study the approach the GottaLearn L&D team took to change organizational culture in chapter 8, including how they shared their work with management in an informal lunch & learn. Look for and celebrate the following OK-LCD principles at work, because these can empower the shift:

- Acknowledge modern L&D accountability for going beyond one-and-done training. Rather than allowing stakeholders and customers to dictate the product L&D delivers, L&D needs to share from their expertise what is needed and what they will provide to meet the gap.
- Refocus everyone on the goal of changing performance. Build confidence in delivering something different by shifting focus from the end product to the goal everyone wants: to change performance on the job.
- Pilot and showcase the results when multiple assets work together to close a gap. Pilot one learning cluster for a learning initiative and share the success. As L&D starts to build momentum based on these early projects, more and more champions of the new approach will emerge in the organization and expectations will change.

Budget

The OK-LCD model helps overcome budget concerns in several ways:

- **Investments are backed by data.** Rather than selecting random technologies to invest in or learning assets to create, L&D can now provide the data to show that learners want it or need it, and through it, business goals will be met (Change and Learn Actions).
- **Sponsorship is gained for future L&D initiatives.** As you've seen in the In Practice sections, once an L&D department has one significant success, budget is usually not an issue. In contrast to budget reduction, demonstrating how L&D is contributing to the business goals invites increased funding. L&D is seen as a critical investment for business performance.

L&D Staffing

Many are initially concerned that creating multiple learning assets will require a significant uptick in resource requirements. However, the reality is that it gets easier and less resource intensive after the first learning cluster. The first one always requires 110 percent because we are in a learning mode. After that, here are the things that reduce staffing effort, or at a minimum, redirect staff efforts:

- Multiple learning assets can reduce design time, because it's faster to design and release products if all the content isn't crammed into one learning asset.
- Crowdsourcing materials means less creation time. Instead, L&D staff focus on providing a template for the crowd to fill out as a way to effectively share knowledge and experience. (Search WikiHow to see how they created standard templates for do-it-yourselfers.)
- Repurpose and reuse learning assets—crowdsourced or L&D-created—for significant time savings.
- Enable peer-to-peer teaching by setting up internal systems, such as blogs and wikis. As you get started on such forms, assign a SME to assure quality feedback to system users and creators.
- Tap into internal partnerships to leverage both staff and budget as you deliver new technologies or set up new infrastructure. L&D organizations have partnered with IT (most common) to design and develop software, piggybacked on software or apps used in operations, and even used client-facing software for internal L&D purposes. In addition, L&D can leverage strengths like branding and graphic design that are common in staff from other functions, such as marketing or external communications.
- Find external channels of top-notch content that you trust. Create an easy path for employees to get to the resources they need outside the company or organization.

L&D Staff Capabilities

Skills need to be continually honed, just as with any role. OK-LCD brings a few big changes:

- **Manage multiple assets.** First, instructional designers need to learn the skill of effectively managing multiple learning assets to meet business and learner needs. Most L&D professionals are used to the world of single, planned learning assets. Handling design considerations that pertain to business goals, multiple learners, and multiple assets is a new skill. L&D leaders must study up on modern learning design principles and philosophies so they can guide and hold their organizations accountable for delivering on the promise of meeting modern learning needs.
- **Widen L&D technical skill sets.** When assets sit outside the formal learning touchpoint, capabilities beyond training and e-learning software become important. Videography, app development, public speaking, video game design, graphic design, coding, and many more may become commonplace as you view the patterns and trends from your learning clusters. You might find that some of these skills are already hidden talents in your organization. Keep on top

of your L&D team members' personal hobbies—you never know what might be helpful for your next learning cluster.

- **Lean into technology partnerships.** Technology is a deeply complex field. L&D can't—and doesn't need to—know it all. Your staff may not know how to create AR or VR, or program the back end of big data analytics platforms. However, when L&D designs modern learning, we must make sure we can serve as intelligent partners to our technology suppliers. When we show up with thorough learner personas and an understanding of the how the nine elements can be enabled by technology, we can provide invaluable information on the user and design requirements and processes suppliers need to complete. And, if the solution doesn't exist out there, you might need to hire talent internally to build infrastructure you need.

New Directions for L&D

Managing change isn't all about overcoming barriers from the way things were done; it's also about introducing and maximizing the new possibilities of the future.

L&D can play a stronger role in performance management and career development. When big data technologies are introduced, your counterparts in performance and career development departments may start to take notice. Every emergent technology, from virtual reality to measurement platforms, is focused on collecting every piece of data as a user moves through the system. Given all we know as L&D experts, you play a role in deciding how to use the data wisely in a way that enables performance rather than hurts the learning experience. Be clear with other company groups that learning cluster data measures learners while they are practicing and learning—these data cannot be used for bonuses or promotion, or to weed out low performers. We have seen evidence of such thinking, thankfully in only a few rare cases. At the same time, data can be used to help learners grow by connecting learners to one another, ensuring access to learning materials, aligning to career goals, and understanding in real time any help needed.

L&D can support change initiatives. In practice, change management often devolves to a communication strategy. L&D, through their persona work and behavior change focus, may be asked to get involved in change initiatives by creating learning clusters to support transitions from old approaches to new. This puts L&D in the center of key business transformations. Start communicating how L&D can serve change efforts and see what the outcomes are!

L&D can serve as a partner for enterprise-wide technology investments. As you build more and more learning clusters, you will begin to see patterns of certain types of technology and infrastructure that will add value to the organization and the organization's learners. You might also see how technology from another function could be used for learning purposes. Get more in the know with the technology the organization is considering and show your support as appropriate.

Envisioning Your Future With the OK-LCD Model

Building your capability in designing modern learning through the OK-LCD model isn't a one-and-done event. It's an iterative, moment-to-moment journey. This book is one asset on your shelf. We hope it has helped you learn in your first moment of learning need: learning for the first time. And, because a book is autonomous and accessible, you can pick it up at any time and refresh your knowledge when you face other moments of learning need. Because books are chunked into chapters and we've interspersed numerous graphics and visual clues throughout, we hope you can find just what you want when you want it.

But a book is just one learning asset. Building a future full of powerful learning clusters isn't a task you have to take on alone. To more fully support your journey to designing modern learning, we've applied our own process to create a learning cluster on the Owens-Kadakia Learning Cluster Design model (Figure 9-3). We also offer learning assets that help upskill you and your colleagues in the language and Actions so you can practice together the next time you take on a learning challenge. We also invite you to collaborate with our expert consultants on your next project, so you can deliver results on the complex challenges you're facing and gain organizational buy-in quickly. Finally, we encourage you to help contribute and grow the modern learning community through our social learning assets. Connecting with modern learning peers and staying in touch with our research helps us as an L&D profession, make this important leap together. You can find it all on LearningClusterDesign.com.

The model, each Action, and the supporting stories that we've shared throughout this book represent an integrated, yet flexible solution to address the many changes facing the L&D industry. Rather than jumping on the bandwagon of flashy and latest trends, we've provided a process for strategic modern learning design. We've provided a model that allows for future technologies unknown today, and avoided prescriptive design recommendations. We continue to encourage L&D to expand their skills and ideas, rather than sticking to the core capabilities that served us in the past.

Disruption has rocked many industries in recent years, and L&D is no exception. Often, we experience change in small pieces, but it's only over time we realize the full picture has transformed. We're left wondering where we stand in a new world. Before we find ourselves looking back, let's move forward bravely, adopting new thinking and new ways that will guide us for the next century. We in L&D have never considered the possibility of delivering multiple assets, tied to one another and tied to business performance. Now the possibility is in your hands. We've provided the philosophy and principles, the model for action, and the tools to help you act. We've left an open door to come collaborate with us and leverage our expertise to make learning clusters a reality in your organization. But, it's up to you to bring modern learning to life. When people grow, so do organizations, and ultimately, so do communities.

Are you ready? Together, let's lead the way and level up talent development.

Figure 9-3. Learning Cluster to Upskill on OK-LCD

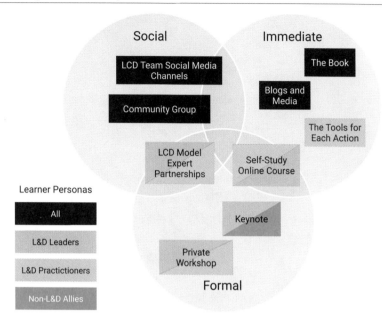

Learning Asset	Learning Asset Description	Where You Can Find It
LCD Team Social Media Channels	For ongoing insights, follow our company. Our team members are great resources you can reach out to with any questions.	LearningClusterDesign.com/about-team
Community Group	As we continue to grow, we are adding new ways for peer-to-peer learning and sharing LCD model success stories. We can all learn together.	LearningClusterDesign.com/community
Blogs and Media	Subscribe to our blog to stay up to date with our latest research.	LearningClusterDesign.com/research
The Book	Keep this book handy and share it with others who want to upskill in modern learning.	td.org/books/Designing-for-Modern-Learning
Keynote	Create a mindset shift on learning and development at your company through a powerful keynote at your next leadership meeting or conference.	LearningClusterDesign.com/contact
Expert Partnerships	The ultimate learning happens when doing. Engage with our LCD model expert consultant team to help deliver business results and develop your capability along the way.	LearningClusterDesign.com/consulting
Self-Study Online Course	Get an introduction to the LCD model for you and your team through our online course.	LearningClusterDesign.com/learning-solutions
Private Workshop	Build foundational capability for your team through a one- or two-day private workshop.	LearningClusterDesign.com/learning-solutions
Tools for Each Action	Use the latest tool templates as a job aid to help execute each Action with success.	LearningClusterDesign.com/book-bonus

Acknowledgments

This book is possible because of collaboration with so many people who provided insights, points of view, opinions, stories, experiences, and more. To all of you, our deepest thanks. Together, we can modernize our profession, now and for the decades to come.

To the Ohio University instructional design students in Lisa's live online master's class who contributed to the language of modern learning and the nine elements of modern learning, especially Chris Hawks, Siyang Jang, Chris Palmer, Tracy Robinson, and Kyle Rosenberger.

To our Designing for Modern Learners workshop participants, especially Amy Bartle, John Cline, Brienne Crouse, Tanacha Clinton, Dawson Cochran, Charles Evans, Sherri Guerra, Steve Hawkins, Kelly Muno, Loc Nguyen, Megan Roddy, and LuAnn Tarvin. To Diane Mullins (then with Good Practice Training Group), Leigh Tingle (then with Bridge Education), Stephen Wallmark (Talent Analytics), and Zach Rubin (Professional Book Club Guru) for supporting our workshop with your materials.

To local ATD chapter members who attended mini sessions on parts of the LCD model and provided additional insights at monthly meetings. Especially at ATD Southwest Florida, Lorna Kibbey, Vern Schellenger, Dulce Gonell, Melissa Rizzuto, and Rebecca Ruding; and at ATD Greater Cincinnati (and Dayton), Leah Cridlin, Carol Erisman, Chris Eversole, Greg Goold, John Healey, Pam Nintrup, Bob Riess, Laurel Sharp, Rita Verderber, Steve Wallmark, Karen Bishea Williams, Otis Williams, and Jonathan Wilson.

People in our network who replied promptly to our many emails asking for opinions on this or that tool or rubric, concept or definition, including Dawson Cochran, Greg Goold, Diane Hartt, Shubhangi Kelkar, Lorna Kibbey, Pam Nintrup, Mike Pino, Tracy Robinson, Eli Thomas, Vern Schellenger, and Agnus White. A special thanks to Karen Bishea Williams who partnered with us to craft major elements of the Learn Tool.

Thank you to those of you who provided your stories for this book: From BlueScape, Loc Nguyen. From Comcast, Martha Soehren, Keith Deangelis, David Barone, Jenna Wisniewski, and Jessica Stubbs. From The Gorilla Glue Company, LuAnn Tarvin and Brienne Crouse. From Paycor, Greg Goold, Maggie Jackson, and Jillian Hintz. Formerly from Zappos, Rich Hazeltine, Amy Stewart, and Allison of Customer Service.

To Tanacha Clinton, a huge thank you! Tanacha contributed her graphics talent, combined with her instructional design expertise to create our learning cluster design model graphic so that the LCD model graphic has a sense of direction while remaining iterative and circular.

Lastly, to our ATD associates, especially Ann Parker who initiated this work and supported us since 2014 with many interactions both virtual and face to face. Also, Clara Von Ins, Eliza Blanchard, Patty Gaul, Kay Hechler, and Steve Earnest. And to our developmental editor Kathryn Stafford, who went so far as to travel out of state to take our two-day course for a deep dive into the LCD concepts. Her enthusiasm and skill have pushed us beyond our initial writing to ensure that the LCD message can be easily devoured by readers like you.

APPENDIX 1
Change On-the-Job Behavior Tool

Objective of This Tool: Articulate the on-the-job change goals (the strategic performance objective) for the learning cluster through a reverse-engineering process, starting with the business results you expect to improve. Obtain inputs for the template through interviews of project stakeholders and customers.

Later, during the Surround Action, form the terminal objectives and enabling objectives to support the learning assets and achieve the strategic performance objective.

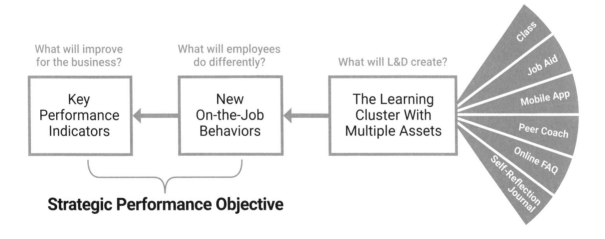

Strategic Performance Objective

By improving _____ for _____,
[Name the skill or performance gap]   [Name the target learner group]

the business will benefit by _____.
[Describe which KPIs will improve, such as cost, volume, competitiveness, time]

The changes to on-the-job behavior that we will see are [List one or more desired observable behaviors]:

-
-
-

During the Surround Action, to complete the objectives hierarchy for your learning cluster, write the terminal and enabling objectives. Use the graphic and templates below as a guide.

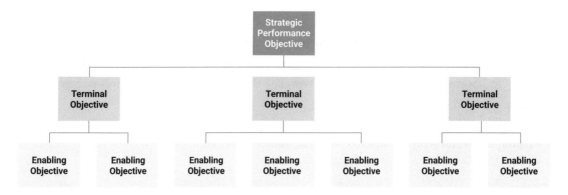

Terminal Performance Objective

This learning asset helps _____ to _____,
[Audience/"who"]   [Behavior/visible skill]

given _____ and do it _____.
[Conditions, situation, job aid, or tools]   [Degree, quality of visible performance]

Enabling Objective

This module or section helps _____ to _____,
[Audience/"who"]   [Behavior/visible skill]

given _____ and do it _____.
[Conditions, situation, job aid, or tools]   [Degree, quality of visible performance]

APPENDIX 2

Learn Learner-to-Learner Differences Tool

Objective of This Tool: Dig deep into understanding the learning-need differences among your target learner group—differences that can influence your choice of learning assets as well as inform your instructional design. This tool guides you as you capture and verbalize these differences. The end result is a set of learner persona stories that characterize unique segments of your learner population relative to the SPO (strategic performance objective).

1. Summarize What You Already Know

Jot down what you already know about this group of learners. A common way to record this information is in table form, but use whatever system meets your need.

Use the learner information list to fill in what you already know. You'll fill in the blank spots in step 2. Start with basic demographic differences among the larger learner group. Add pertinent differences that you glean from previous experience or from early discussions with stakeholders or others who asked for this learning cluster. Importantly, note your early suspicions about which subsets within your target learner group have a greater impact on the desired KPI described in the SPO. Ask yourself:

- Who has the biggest performance gap ("problem approach")?
- Whose growth would significantly influence the whole ("strengths" approach)?

   Tip: Be bold. These data are for your eyes only. If you know what the problem child is, name it! Indentifying obvious realities and barriers is a good way to ensure they're addressed effectively.

Keep in mind that you're searching for key differences among subsets of the larger learner group. *Key* means relevant to this project, SPO, and skill gap, or desired on-the-job behavior and performance. Don't try to collect every scrap of data. That'd be overwhelming!

2. Dig Deeper Into Learner Differences

Identify Additional Information Needs. As in step 1, use the following list to gather crucial information. To uncover important learner-to-learner differences, seek out data that will:

- Reveal learner-to-learner differences that affect what, where, when, and how these learners need to learn.
- Expose differences in skills, attitudes, and knowledge.
- Underscore differences in current performance and differential impact on the SPO.
- Confirm or refute your "Already Know" information noted in step 1.

How will you get your data? Some common methods used to collect both qualitative and quantitative data include interviews, surveys, observation on the job, self-assessments, tests, and analysis of existing work or data. Sometimes data collection will be a budget item. Other times this information already exists within the company, just waiting for your analysis.

Learner Information to Support Discovering Differences

Most learning projects benefit from the following data. You may need additional items to support the work on your learning project. Be aware that you are trying to find enough data to identify subsets within your larger learner group, not collect all the information known about them.

◊ Key Demographic Differences
- List only what is pertinent to this SPO, the skill gap, the KPIs, and desired on-the-job behavior.
- Examples: role, function, level, tenure, age, gender, division, country

◊ Key Learning Need Differences (in General)
- Typical response to training or learning
- Primary technology used on the job (as a go-to for learning assets or performance support)
- Preferred learning go-tos (example, class, e-learning, video, self-assessments)
- Level of self-awareness

◊ Key Life-at-Work Differences (in General)
- Work hours
- Job environment
- Level of discretionary time
- Best time for learning (away from desk, during meetings, at home)
- Barriers to learning
- Network for learning (whom do they go to for answers?)

◊ Key Performance Gap Differences (Specific to Project)
- Current skill or performance level
- Attitude toward this skill set
- Barriers to behavior change
- Awareness of this skill set, or the need for it on the job
- Self-assessment of capability for this skill set
- Estimated impact on KPIs
- Who has the biggest performance gap ("problem approach")?
- Whose growth would significantly influence the whole ("strengths" approach)?

◊ Likely moments of learning need: Which moments are learners likely to face; where and when will they face these moments?
- Learning for the first time (new)
- Learning more
- Applying what was learned
- When things go wrong
- When things change

◊ Ideas about the types of learning assets that might appeal or be needed

3. Analyze to Create Learner Persona Profiles

Do the analysis soon after information collection. Letting time lapse muddies impressions, and you miss out on important aha moments. During the analysis, be data-driven, avoid early judgments, and minimize bias and personal preferences. It's helpful to form a hypothesis, then use the data to prove or disprove the idea.

As you complete the information analysis, pull from it three to five personas, and complete a profile for each. The following table is a good starting place. Fill in the left column with what you chose to gather, but only if it's pertinent to painting a picture of differences between the personas. A few rows are filled in for you and are highly recommended for every project.

> **Tip:** You do not have to include polar opposites for each persona, just the ones that strongly influence the SPO. For example, if "newly promoted" is a group, your other personas should be deeper than "promoted long ago."

For more help on data analysis, see "The Art of Knowledge Analysis for Creating Learner Personas."

Learner Persona Profiles

Persona Name Short summary description	1.	2.	3.
Likely impact on SPO (high, medium, low)			
1. Key Demographic Differences			
2. Key Learning-Need Differences			
Typical response to training and learning			
Primary technology used on the job			
Preferred learning go-tos			
Attitude at work			
3. Key Life-at-Work Differences			
4. Key Performance Gap Differences			
Current skill or performance level			
5. Moments of Learning Need			

4. Create the Learner Personas Stories

Write a creative explanatory story for each persona. To bring the story to life, be sure to name your persona and give it a face—literally—using an avatar or other facial image. Just start, then fine-tune. Test the personas with others. Do the characteristics feel true? When read as a group, key differences should be obvious. The connection between each persona and the SPO and skill gaps should be clear and distinctive. These stories serve as a foundation for selecting learning assets for the learning cluster to meet the learning and performance needs of each persona. You can use these to justify your selection of learning assets as part of the learning cluster.

Persona 1

Persona 2

Persona 3

Persona 4

5. Use the Persona to Guide Learning Asset Selection and Design

Thinking about one persona at a time, jot down what learning assets would help to build skill, reduce frustration, and be present in learners' moment of learning need. Refer to the persona's story and profile regularly through out this process. The following chart is one way to brainstorm and capture it. During the Surround Action, learning assets will be chosen, and this chart will be a great guide!

Learning Assets That Could Meet the Learner Persona Needs

Persona 1: _____	Persona 2: _____	Persona 3: _____
•	•	•
•	•	•
•	•	•

The Art of Knowledge Analysis for Creating Learning Personas

Now that you've captured all the data, it's time to analyze them. Karen Bishea, a persona expert, says, "This is done best as a team exercise. You can do it electronically, but in my experience, using poster-sized templates posted all around the room helps to capture the big key learning in a visual format that promotes discovery."

- Study the information.
- Lay the foundation—create knowledge grids from demographics, interviews, and survey knowledge.
- Create persona outline drafts through information assessment, evaluation, and plotting of knowledge. Seek three to five different personas.
- Start to visualize each persona. It helps to organize and prioritize items from the outline draft. Have faith—this is the hard part.
- Start to paint the picture of each persona with words. This process creates additional insights, connections, and relationships.
- Step back, view holistically, and adjust as needed. Each persona should describe not an individual, but a composite of individuals.
- Finalize your three to five persona profiles, adding or refining words to elicit a mental image.

Not coming together? Here are some approaches:

- Take a break, then try again. Artists need subconscious processing time.
- In some cases, scrap it and restart with a fresh piece of paper, remembering to use your information to drive your conclusions.
- Test your drafts with someone outside the group to gain insights.

For more on Learner Personas, see the *TD at Work* issue "Learner Personas: Beyond Demographics," written by Karen Bishea, who collaborated with the authors on this tool.

APPENDIX 3

Upgrade the Existing Tool

Objective of This Tool: Modernize existing learning assets or create new ones by strategically adding ways to include the nine elements in your asset.

Instructions:

1. Give a descriptive name for the learning asset you want to modernize. In the step 1 column, enter "1" or "0" in the cells if the asset has (1) or does not have (0) each modernness element. Sum the column.

2. Is it possible for the asset to include this element? Enter yes or no in the step 2 column. (Think creatively.)

3. The step 3 column describes ideas on how to include this element. List all ideas; don't limit yourself at this stage based on money, resources, etc. Consider the values and motivators for your learner personas that you visualized in the Learn Tool. Use the comments column to note any details.

4. Are ideas feasible now or later? (Later means needs additional resources—cost, time, staff—that aren't available now.) Indicate N (now) or or L (later) in the step 4 column.

5. Highlight ideas from the step 4 column that you are willing and able to accomplish as part of your modernized learning asset. Create a descriptive name for this set of choices and enter the name below the chart. Next, give your new asset a modernness score, by entering 1 or 0 to indicate which elements are included. Sum this column to get your new modernness score. Is your new modernness score a few points higher than the score for your existing asset? Hurray! You can do it!

Note: This tool may encourage ideas for new learning assets. See the Surround Action for how to include these in your learning cluster.

Upgrade the Existing Tool

Existing asset: _____

[Name of asset]

	Step 1: Rate Existing (1=Yes; 0=No)	Step 2: Possible? (Y/N)	Step 3: List Ideas for This Element	Step 4: Now or Later?	Step 5: Rate Modernized Option (1=Yes; 0=No)	Modernized Asset Description: (List to do "now" modernization plans here)
Nine Elements of a Modern Learning Asset						**Comments**
Accessible						
Autonomous						
Chunked						
Current						
Experiential						
For Me						
Hyperlinked						
MVAK						
Social						
Modernness Score						

Modernized asset: _____

[Name of asset]

What is your modernized difference? _____

[Sum of step 1 – sum of step 5]

APPENDIX 4

Surround Learners With Meaningful Assets Tool

Objective of This Tool: Take the modern way to closing skills gaps by providing multiple learning assets across all three learning touchpoints (social, formal, and immediate) in a deliberate, thoughtful way, which ensures learning content is available at key moments of learning need.

1. **Name of Learning Cluster:** _____

   [usually name of performance improvement goal]

2. **SPO** *(Change Action)*: By improving _____ for _____,

   [skill]   [learner group]

   the business will benefit by _____. The changes to on-the-job behavior that

   [KPIs]

   we will see among team members include _____.

   [visible behaviors on the job]

3. **Learning Asset Types by Learner Personas** *(from Learn Action and Upgrade Action)*:

_____ (Persona 1)	_____ (Persona 2)	_____ (Persona 3)	All

4. Learning Cluster Development

- **Brainstorm.** Consider each learner persona, one by one, and brainstorm learning assets that have potential for meeting the unique needs of each persona—when, where, and how they work and learn. No single asset will cover all terminal and enabling learning objectives, but the entire column of assets will address the learning objectives needed by this persona.
  - In the chart, under the persona name, enter the name of the asset (usually based on media, such as video, class, wiki object, or e-learning).
  - Describe each learning asset to communicate the idea within that cell.
  - Work down each column. Some assets may appear in more than one column.
  - Use results from the first three Actions as input for this brainstorming session.
- **Converge.** Looking at the entire set of possible learning assets, select those you want to include in this learning cluster. Consider the learning needs of each persona, as well as what is realistic for your situation. This may take several rounds of trial and error to find the right mix.
- **Map assets to learning touchpoints.** Each persona should have an asset in each touchpoint:
  - For each selected asset, copy the short name into a box or cell of the appropriate color.
  - Move colored boxes to a suitable location on the learning cluster visual.
  - Assets that work for all personas are in black and white (delete duplicates).
  - Missing something? Identify additional assets to meet the learner persona need.

  Tip: Resulting image should be a mix of color and B&W (for all), rarely all B&W.

- **Check and recheck**
  - Do you have a learning asset for each learning touchpoint for each persona?
  - Are there any needs uncovered from your learner personas that are not being met?
  - Do the assets further the strategic performance objective for your learning cluster?

5. **Assign Terminal and Enabling Objectives to Each Learning Asset.** Return to the hierarchical relationship of objectives as shown in the Change Tool. List the terminal objectives and enabling objectives to the level of detail required for this project. Indicate which learning assets will cover each objective. Ensure that learners will be exposed to learning assets for each objective relevant to that persona, and provide choices to help them reach these learning objectives when, where, and how they need to learn. (Employ your usual learning objective mapping tools, modifying as needed to accomplish this step.)

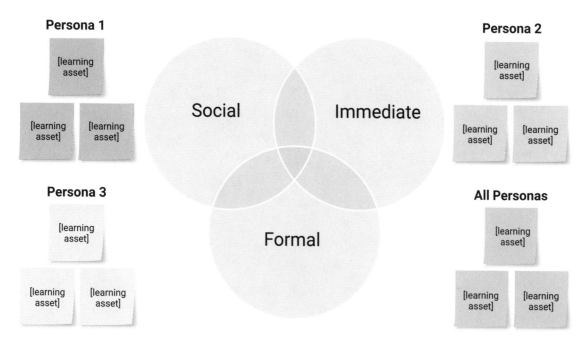

APPENDIX 5

Track Transformation of Everyone's Results Tool

Objective of This Tool: Measure your learning cluster's overall effect on changing learners' on-the-job behavior, and positive changes in select KPIs. Additionally, seek out powerful stories that exemplify the learning cluster's impact. Lastly, gather some measures for key learning assets to ensure that L&D is working effectively. (Note: This tool is focused on measuring the impact of the learning cluster. Overall L&D effectiveness, as a result of adopting the OK-LCD model, is addressed separately.) With these measures, L&D can:

- Articulate meaningful goals and targets so that learners, L&D, and the business know the "finish line" that they are targeting.
- Demonstrate value that invites further support through funding and business resources.
- Provide internal feedback so L&D knows what is working for learners and what needs improvement.

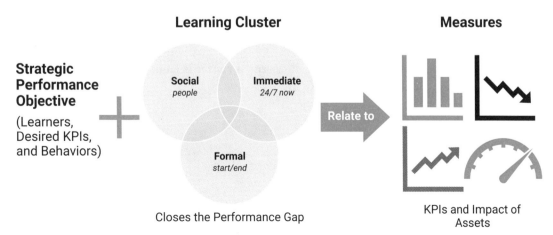

Learning Cluster Name: _____

Learning Cluster Strategic Performance Objectives:

Step 1: Select Measures for the Overall Learning Cluster

The purpose of this set of measures is to determine if the approach is working. Can you identify a trend as you build a critical mass of employees who are changing their behavior such that the KPIs improve?

What Is Measured	How to Get Data	Pre-Cluster Value	Goal	Post-Cluster Value
KPI: _____				
Behavior 1				
Behavior 2				

- In the first column, list the KPI measures and desired on-the-job behavior changes that this learning cluster is designed to impact, as called out in the SPO.
- Determine how L&D can obtain these data regularly. (This may take some work and negotiation.)
- Get a baseline measure wherever possible (the value of the KPI or measure of the behavior before the learning cluster is introduced).
- Determine the goal (for example, percentage change, specific value, evidence gathered through anecdotal stories). Note a timeframe for this change (a week, quarter, year?).

Save the right column for later. Fill it in after the learning cluster is launched. Periodically gather the data and compare results with the goal (column 4).

Step 2: Measures for Key Learning Assets

The purpose of this set of measures is to determine if L&D is meeting learner needs and to identify assets whose metrics share a story that gets attention.

Learning Asset	SFI	Metric	Kirkpatrick Level 1–4	Goal	How and When to Get the Data
Example: mentoring program	S	1. % mentees agree mentor helps them perform better 2. testimony from mentees and mentors on their experience	3	1. 70% top 2 box 2. two good stories a quarter	Quarterly 2-question survey of active mentee/mentor pairs. (80% response rate)

- List key learning assets in the following table (group similar ones, like sets of videos).
- Note the learning touchpoints for the asset.
- Choose metrics for each learning asset or group of similar assets. It may take some brainstorming and discussion to arrive at a decision. Consider:
  - How do learners demonstrate performance with this asset? (During or after use? Through Q&A?)
  - What groups will contribute to the measure. Learner only or others?
- Note which Kirkpatrick level of evaluation this measure looks at. Try for a mix of levels (not just Level 1 or Level 2).
- Jot down the goal. This may be tough because then L&D is committed, but without a goal, we don't know when we've reached the finish line and can declare success.
- Determine how to get the measure and on what frequency. Be realistic, and consider how long this measure will need to be in place.

Step 3: Select a Few to Share

Choose a few measures in step 1 and 2. For L&D purposes you want to measure all assets and overall effects, but for a management summary we need a more concise story. Choose from the previous measures what could be the most powerful to inspire stakeholders and employees to recommend this learning cluster. Make sure to include at least one measure from step 1.

-

-

-

-

Over time, you might rotate measures or find that a particular asset is contributing to the SPO. Change the story as needed to continue to show the relevance and contribution of a modern L&D.

Example

Learning Cluster Name: Continuous Feedback

Learning Cluster Strategic Performance Objective:

By improving *continuous feedback skills* for *managers of others (experienced* and *new-to-role)*, the business will benefit by *improving new hire time-to-productivity and employee engagement.* The changes to on-the-job behavior will include *frequent feedback conversations that follow the selected feedback model.*

Learning Asset	SFI	Metric	Kirkpatrick Level 1–4	Goal	How and When to Get the Data
Learning Cluster	SFI	• Time to productivity • Annual survey; feedback questions • Employee engagement	4, 5 3 4, 5	• ↑ 10% • 60% top two-box • ↑ 5%	Year-to-year change
Manager Community of Practice (online)	S	• # of posts/month • Review posts for stories	2, 3	• 15% write • 60% look	• Report from website • Read posts online
Direct Report Feedback	SF	• Survey 20% of direct reports	3	• Trends Up, Goal = 75	
App Reminder or Journal	I	• Percentage users • Uses per month	2, 3	• 60% use • Avg. twice monthly	Report from website
Bite-Size Videos	SI	• # of thumbs-up or down • See comments for stories	1, 3	• 10% click, • 3 stories/yr	Report from website
Self-Assessment Tool	I	80% use 2+ times/year	3		Report from website
Classroom	SF	• Smile sheets • Trainer assessment	1, 2 2	• 80% T2B • 80%	• LMS summary • LMS questionnaire

Glossary

Action: Describes an L&D activity and responsibility as a part of engaging in and executing the OK-LCD model for modern learning design.

> **Action, Change On-the-Job Behavior (Change Action)** is focused on setting the target goal (or **strategic performance objective**) for the overall process, specifically to affect employees' performance in their day-to-day work. This is one of three early Actions leading to the Surround Action.

> **Action, Learn Learner-to-Learner Differences (Learn Action)** is focused on investigating nuances within the target learner group of the effort, particularly those nuances that contribute to meeting the target goal. This is one of three early Actions leading to the Surround Action.

> **Action, Upgrade Existing Assets (Upgrade Action)** is focused on applying the nine elements of modern learning to improve current programs quickly and effectively. This is one of three early Actions leading to the Surround Action.

> **Action, Surround Learners With Meaningful Assets (Surround Action)** is focused on selecting learning assets to subsequently design, based on the inputs of the first three early Actions.

> **Action, Track Transformation for Everyone's Results (Track Action)** is focused on evaluating the impact of the learning cluster, with a particular emphasis on Levels 3 and 4 of the Kirkpatrick model. This is the last Action of the model, but the process continues as feedback from evaluation inspires review of previous Actions.

AGES Model for Learning: A neuroscience-based learning theory that outlines the four requirements for the brain to learn: attention, generation, emotion, and spacing.

Artificial Intelligence: Technology that gives machines the capability to recognize and respond to image, sound, and language inputs.

Augmented Reality (AR): An interactive experience of a real-world environment where the objects that reside in the real world are enhanced by computer-generated perceptual information, sometimes across multiple sensory modalities.

Big Data: Extremely large data sets that may be analyzed computationally to reveal patterns, trends, and associations, especially relating to human behavior and interactions.

Chatbot: a computer program designed to simulate conversation with human users, especially over the Internet.

Course or **Training:** A set of content with a structured sequence between the start and finish that is intended to close a skill or competency gap.

Curation: From marketing expert Rohit Bhargava: "A content curator is someone who continually finds, groups, organizes, and shares the best and most relevant content on a specific issue." For L&D professionals, to leverage the scale of your organization is to curate the best content from in-company experts. A second way to curate content is to allow users to rate valuable content, both inside and outside company boundaries.

Five Moments of Learning Need: A learning theory from researchers Bob Mosher and Conrad Gottfredson that describes the five occasions that drive a person to seek learning.

Instructional Models: Offer a way for instructional designers to effectively collect the information needed, organize the content well, and brainstorm ways to deliver the learning. They are grounded in, but are not the same as, **learning theories**.

Key Performance Indicator (KPI): Business metric used to evaluate factors that are crucial to the success of an organization. KPIs differ by organization; business KPIs may be net revenue or a customer loyalty metric, while government might consider unemployment rates.

Kirkpatrick Levels of Evaluation: A model for evaluating training that Donald Kirkpatrick is credited with pioneering in 1959. The model has four evaluation steps: reaction, learning, behavior, and results.

Learner: A person, such as a participant or an employee, who wants to change actions or skills.

Learner Persona: A descriptive story of a subgroup within your target learner group that relays the key differences in demographics, learning needs, life at work, performance gaps, and most likely moments of learning need.

Learning: The process of taking in information or content, making sense of it, and applying it.

Learning Asset: A general term describing a wide range of things that help people learn. It might be content to read, an online search, a class (face-to-face or online), a discussion, a video, or even a motivational poster. It can be as small as a 30-second audio recording or as large as a three-month class. In traditional training, a learning asset most often takes the form of a class, an e-learning course, or a blended learning program.

Learning Cluster: A set of learning assets intended to address a specific performance gap across multiple contexts, which we call **learning touchpoints**.

Learning Theory: A research-grounded attempt to describe how humans assimilate, process, and retain information.

Learning Touchpoints: The points of contact between modern learners and how they get the knowledge they need in the way that they need it to succeed in their work. These can be tagged as having characteristics that are social, formal, and immediate.

> **Learning Touchpoint, Formal:** Instance of learning in which learners experience a clear start and end point, often a structured sequence or path to follow through content, and often ending with a completion certificate. Historically, L&D provides formal learning touchpoints. These are often recorded in the employee's record or on a learning management system (LMS). Typical examples include classes, courses, e-learning modules, and certificate programs, but may also include prescribed job rotation plans, blended learning, and action learning programs.

> **Learning Touchpoint, Immediate:** Instance of learning in which learners' experience includes 24/7 access and availability in the moment, without extensive searching. Typically, this is material online in the form of job aids, wikis, searchable databases, active discussion boards, or menu-driven, bite-sized e-learning content.

> **Learning Touchpoint, Social:** Instance of learning in which learners have a level of interaction with other people. This includes, but is not limited to, user-generated content; likes, views, and comments; face-to-face interaction; mentoring; coaching; and dialogue among peers.

Microlearning: Learning elements that are intentionally designed to be bite-sized, whether in the formal, social, or immediate category.

Net Promoter Score (NPS): An index ranging from -100 to 100 that measures the willingness of customers to recommend a company's products or services to others. It is used as a proxy for gauging the customer's overall satisfaction with a company's product or service and the customer's loyalty to the brand.

Nine Elements of Modern Learning: These are the elements that are found more frequently in learning methods that are perceived as modern. They include:

- **Accessible:** Easy to find, and available in the moment
- **Autonomous:** Self-directed and able to be completed without help
- **Chunked:** Content presented in small divisions (such as two-minute videos, 20-minute talking head, five text paragraphs)
- **Current:** Up-to-date or easily updatable (by author or others)
- **Experiential:** Something is done, with feedback, sometimes immediately
- **For Me:** Curated and delivered based on learners' preferences
- **Hyperlinked:** Linked to content that is more basic, in-depth, or current
- **MVAK:** Multimedia providing input that is visual, auditory, or kinesthetic
- **Social:** Includes other people through crowdsourcing, likes, views, or comments; or includes face-to-face interaction in classes and through coaching, mentoring, or dialogue.

Owens-Kadakia Learning Cluster Design (OK-LCD) Model: An intentional, context-centered instructional development approach to selecting, designing, and facilitating access to a set of learning assets to improve performance on-the-job for a particular capability. It is both a philosophy (way of thinking), described by four **principles**, and a process (a way of doing), described by five **Actions**.

OK-LCD Model Principles describe L&D's new job and the way of thinking necessary to effectively implement the OK-LCD model:

> **Go Beyond One-and-Done:** L&D's new role is to deliver and facilitate access to multiple learning assets, not one asset, per capability gap.

> **Design the Whole, Not the Parts:** Multiple learning assets must be viewed and designed as part of an integrated whole, during both design and development of the user experience. They must not be created ad hoc, with lack of consideration for one another.

> **Focus on Learner Needs:** Whereas in the past L&D had limited tools to deliver learning, today we can deliver learning when, where, and how the learner needs it. The design must reflect a deep understanding of the learner and their capability gap first.

> **Change On-the-Job Behavior:** L&D can and should be held accountable for improving performance on the job, not just at the end of a classroom training, course, or program. Improved performance means that there will be a change in behavior through application of knowledge on the job, rather than simply acquiring the knowledge in the program.

Skills Gap: Inability to do a desired task as a result of lack of awareness, information, experience, confidence, desire, or a habit gap (it's about not only learning, but also performing).

Strategic Performance Objective (SPO): The goal for the **learning cluster**, including its full set of **learning assets**. It explains the connection between the business strategy (as described by **key performance indicators**) to the on-the-job behaviors that are expected to improve as a result of the effort.

Target Learner Group: Refers to the general audience of the learning cluster and replaces the historical term *target audience*.

Terminal Objective: The objective or set of objectives that describes expected learner performance at the end of a single learning asset.

Virtual Reality (VR): A computer-generated simulation of a three-dimensional image or environment that can be interacted with in a seemingly real or physical way by a person using special electronic equipment, such as a helmet with a screen inside or gloves fitted with sensors.

Further Reading

Austin, T. 2018. "HR Considerations for Remote Employees." GMS, August 20. groupmgmt.com/blog /post/2018/08/20/HR-Considerations-for-Remote-Employees.aspx.

Benko, C., T. Gorman, and A.R. Steinberg. 2014. "Disrupting the CHRO: Following in the CFO's Footsteps." *Deloitte Review*, 14. deloitte.com/us/en/insights/deloitte-review/issue-14/dr14 -disrupting-the-chro.html.

Boileau, T. n.d. "Informal Learning." In *Foundations of Learning and Instructional Design Technology,* edited by Richard E. West. lidtfoundations.pressbooks.com/chapter/informal-learning-by-boileau.

Change Factory. n.d. "Training Needs Analysis." Change Factory. changefactory.com.au/service /developing-people/training-needs-analysis.

Docebo. 2019. *E-Learning Trends 2019.* Docebo. docebo.com/resource/report-elearning-trends-2019.

Ebbinghaus, H. 1885. *Memory: A Contribution to Experimental Psychology.* New York: Dover.

Edutopia. 2011. "Resources on Learning and the Brain." Edutopia, October 25. edutopia.org/article /brain-based-learning-resources.

Grovo. 2015. "Training the Trainer: How to Create Microlearning." Whitepaper. Elearning Guild, January 26. elearningguild.com/sponsored/56/training-the-trainer-how-to-create-microlearning.

Grovo. 2016. "The Disappearing Act: Why Millennials Leave Companies—And How L&D Can Entice Them to Stay." Whitepaper. Grovo. a1.grovo.com/asset/whitepapers/why-millennials-leave -companies-whitepaper.pdf.

Gutierrez, K. 2016. "10 Statistics on Corporate Training and What They Mean for Your Company's Future." Shift Learning, January 28. shiftelearning.com/blog/statistics-on-corporate-training -and-what-they-mean-for-your-companys-future.

Hart, J. 2015. "The L&D World Is Splitting in Two." Learning in the Modern Workplace, November 12. c4lpt.co.uk/blog/2015/11/12/the-ld-world-is-splitting-in-two.

Hofmann, J. 2004. *Live and Online! Tips, Techniques, and Ready-to-Use Activities for the Virtual Classroom.* San Francisco: Pfeiffer.

National Research Council. 2000. "Mind and Brain." Chapter 5 in *How People Learn: Brain, Mind, Experience, and School: Expanded Edition,* edited by J.D. Bransford, A.L. Brown, and R.R. Cocking. Washington, D.C.: The National Academies Press. nap.edu/read/9853/chapter/8#116.

Klein, A. 2015. "Don't Only Focus on Training—Address Barriers to Performance." Caveo Learning, June 30. caveolearning.com/blog/address-barriers-to-performance.

LinkedIn. 2019. "LinkedIn Workplace Learning Report." LinkedIn. learning.linkedin.com/content /dam/me/business/en-us/amp/learning-solutions/images/workplace-learning-report-2019/pdf /workplace-learning-report-2019.pdf.

Lombardo, M.M., and R.W. Eichinger. 1996. *The Career Architect Development Planner*, 1st ed. Minneapolis: Lominger.

Lombardozzi, C. 2015. "Surprise: New Employees Want Formal Training." ATD Insights, December 7. td.org/insights/surprise-new-employees-want-formal-training.

Origin Learning. 2015. "Blended Learning to Address the Five Moments of Need Infographic." Origin Learning, February 20. blog.originlearning.com/using-blended-learning-to-address-the-five -moments-of-need.

Palmer, K., and D. Blake. 2018. "Developing Employees: How to Help Your Employees Learn From Each Other." *Harvard business Review,* November. hbr.org/2018/11/how-to-help-your -employees-learn-from-each-other.

Paul, K. 2007. *Study Smarter, Not Harder.* Bellingham, WA: Self-Counsel Press.

Performcorp. 2012. "L&D Myopia." Performcorp, July 10. performcorp.wordpress.com/2012/07/10 /l-d-myopia.

Phillips, J.J., and P.P. Phillips. 2016. "Create an Executive-Friendly Learning Scorecard." *Chief Learning Officer,* April 6. chieflearningofficer.com/2016/04/06/create-an-executive-friendly-learning -scorecard.

Quora. 2017. "What Makes Chunking Such an Effective Way to Learn?" *Forbes,* November 8. forbes.com/sites/quora/2017/11/08/what-makes-chunking-such-an-effective-way-to-learn /#77580de160a9.

Rich, K. 2015. "State of Employee Training." Intrado, October 14.

Schimanke, F., F. Hallay, R. Mertens, O. Vornberger, and A. Enders. 2015. "Using a Spaced-Repetition-Based Mobile Learning Game in Database Lectures." Paper presented at World Conference on E-Learning, Kona, HI. researchgate.net/publication/292151229_Using_a_Spaced-Repetition -Based_Mobile_Learning_Game_in_Database_Lectures.

Schimanke, F., R. Mertens, and O. Vornberger. 2013. "What to Learn Next? Content Selection Support in Mobile Game-Based Learning." Paper presented at World Conference on E-Learning, Las Vegas, NV, October. researchgate.net/publication/261952026_WHAT_TO_LEARN_NEXT _CONTENT_SELECTION_SUPPORT_IN_MOBILE_GAME-BASED_LEARNING.

Site Staff. 2012. "Informal Learning: Accidental vs. Intentional. *Chief Learning Officer,* June 14. chieflearningofficer.com/2012/06/14/informal-learning-accidental-vs-intentional.

The Training & Development World. 2019. "Myths and 'Lies' About Training and Learning." The Training & Development World, August 22. thetrainingworld.com/resources/Lies_Myths_and _Misconceptions_About_Learning_and_Instruction.

Vance, D. 2016. "Bring Standards to the Learning Profession." *Chief Learning Officer,* April 12. chieflearningofficer.com/2016/04/12/bring-standards-to-the-learning-profession.

Vance, D., and P. Parskey. 2014. "Managing Learning Like a Business to Deliver Greater Impact, Effectiveness, and Efficiency." Whitepaper. Center for Talent Reporting, July 1. centerfortalentreporting.org/documents/whitepaper-executive-brief.pdf.

WikiHow. 2019. "How to Learn Any Subject Without Teachers." wikihow.com/Learn-Any-Subject -Without-Teachers.

References

Arets, J., C. Jennings, and V. Heijnen. 2016. *702010: Towards 100% performance*. Maastricht: Sutler Media.

Basarab, D. 2011. *Predictive Evaluation: Ensuring Training Delivers Business and Organizational Results*. San Francisco: Berrett-Koehler.

Benko, C., T. Gorman, and A.R. Steinberg. 2014. "Disrupting the CHRO: Following in the CFO's Footsteps." *Deloitte Review,* 14. deloitte.com/insights/us/en/deloitte-review/issue-14/dr14-disrupting -the-chro.html.

Bloom, B.S., G.F. Madaus, and J.T. Hastings. 1981. *Evaluation to Improve Learning.* New York: McGraw-Hill.

Bloom, N., J. Liang, J. Roberts, and J.Y. Zichun. 2015. "Does Working From Home Work? Evidence From a Chinese Experiment." *The Quarterly Journal of Economics 130(1): 165-218.* nbloom.people. stanford.edu/sites/g/files/sbiybj4746/f/wfh.pdf.

Box, G.E.P. 1976. "Science and Statistics." *Journal of the American Statistical Association* 71:791–799. doi:10.1080/01621459.1976.10480949.

Brown, J.S., A. Collins, and P. Duguid. 1989. "Situated Cognition and the Culture of Learning." *Educational Researcher* 18(1): 32–42.

Cermak, J., and M. McGurk. 2010. "Putting a Value on Training." *Mckinsey,* July. mckinsey.com /business-functions/organization/our-insights/putting-a-value-on-training.

Clark, D. 2014. "Spaced-Practice: Free White Paper & 10 Practical Ways to Make It Happen." Learningpool, September 10. donaldclarkplanb.blogspot.com/2014/09/spaced-practice-8 -practical-ways-to.html.

Davachi, L., T. Kiefer, D. Rock, and L. Rock. 2010. "Learning That Lasts Through AGES: Maximizing the Effectiveness of Learning Initiatives." *NeuroLeadership Journal* 3:53-63. blueroom.neuroleadership.com/assets/documents/AGES.pdf.

Davis, J., M. Balda, D. Rock, P. McGinniss, and L. Davachi. 2014. *The Science of Making Learning Stick: An Update to the AGES Model.* NeuroLeadership Institute, August 15. neuroleadership.com /portfolio-items/the-science-of-making-learning-stick-an-update-to-the-ages-model.

Degreed. 2016. *How the Workforce Learns in 2016.* Degreed. get.degreed.com/hubfs/Degreed_How_the _Workforce_Learns_in_2016.pdf.

Deloitte. 2017. "Deloitte Global Human Capital Trends: Rewriting the Rules for the Digital Age." Deloitte. deloitte.com/content/dam/Deloitte/global/Documents/About-Deloitte/central-europe /ce-global-human-capital-trends.pdf.

Encyclopaedia Britannica. 2019. "Moore's Law." Encyclopaedia Britannica, March 29. britannica.com /technology/Moores-law.

Gagné, R.M. 1965. *The Conditions of Learning and Theory of Instruction.* New York: Holt, Rinehart, and Winston.

Giossos, Y., M. Koutsouba, A. Lionarakis, and K. Skavantzos. 2009. "Reconsidering Moore's Transactional Distance Theory." *European Journal of Open, Distance and E-Learning.* eurodl.org/?p=archives&year=2009&halfyear=2&article=374.

Gottfredson, C., and B. Mosher. 2011. *Innovative Performance Support: Strategies and Practices for Learning in the Workflow.* New York: McGraw-Hill.

Greany, K. 2018. "Profile of a Modern Learner [Infographic]." Elucidat, August 15. elucidat.com/blog/modern-learner-profile-infographic.

Gustafson, K.L., and R.M. Branch. 2002. *Survey of Instructional Development Models.* 4th ed. Syracuse, NY: ERIC Clearinghouse on Information and Terminology.

International Workplace Group. 2019. *Welcome to Generation Flex—the Employee Power Shift.* International Workplace Group, March. iwgplc.com/global-workspace-survey-2019.

Jennings, C., V. Heijnen, and J. Arets. 2019. 5 "Myths About the 70:20:10 Reference Model." 70:20:10 Institute, April 12. 702010institute.com/5-myths-702010-reference-model.

Kemp, J.E. 1985. *The Instructional Design Process.* New York: Harper & Row.

Kemp, J.E., G.R. Morrison, and S.V. Ross. 1994. *Design Effective Instruction.* New York: Macmillan.

Kirkpatrick, J.D., and W.K. Kirkpatrick. 2016. *Kirkpatrick's Four Levels of Training Evaluation.* Alexandria, VA: ATD Press.

Kirkpatrick Partners. n.d. "Our Philosophy: The Kirkpatrick Model." Kirkpatrick Partners. kirkpatrickpartners.com/Our-Philosophy/The-Kirkpatrick-Model.

Knowles, M.S. 1968. "Andragogy, Not Pedagogy." *Adult Leadership* 16(10): 350–352, 386.

LinkedIn. 2017. "LinkedIn Workplace Learning Report." LinkedIn. learning.linkedin.com/resources/workplace-learning-report-2018#. (Note that the 2017 report has been removed from the website.)

Mager, R. 1972. *Goal Analysis.* Belmont, CA: Fearon Publishers.

Mauer, R. 2019. "HR and Chatbots Are Learning Together. Society for Human Resource Management, April 30. shrm.org/ResourcesAndTools/hr-topics/technology/Pages/HR-Chatbots-Are-Learning-Together.aspx.

Moore, M. 1997. "Theory of Transactional Distance." Chapter 2 in *Theoretical Principles of Distance Education*, edited by D. Keegen, 22–38. New York: Routledge.

Mosher, B., and C. Gottfredson. 2012. "Are You Meeting All Five Moments of Learning Need?" Learning Solutions, June 18. learningsolutionsmag.com/articles/949/are-you-meeting-all-five-moments-of-learning-need.

Reichheld, F. 2003. "The One Number You Need to Grow." *Harvard Business Review,* December. hbr.org/2003/12/the-one-number-you-need-to-grow.

Rich, K. 2015. "State of Employee Training (Infographic)." Intrado, October 14. westuc.com/en-us/blog/webinars-enterprise-streaming/state-employee-training-infographic.

ROI Institute. n.d. "Free Tools." ROI Institute. roiinstitute.net/download/response-to-linkedin-post.

SAS. 2019. "Artificial Intelligence: What It Is and Why It Matters." SAS. sas.com/en_us/insights/analytics/what-is-artificial-intelligence.html.

Seidman, D. 2014. "From the Knowledge Economy to the Human Economy." *Harvard Business Review*, November 12. hbr.org/2014/11/from-the-knowledge-economy-to-the-human-economy

Soehren, M. 2019. "It's All About the Impact." *TD* Magazine, June.

Staron, L. 2018. "Employee Training and Development: How to Measure the ROI of Training Programs." HR Technologist, September 11. hrtechnologist.com/articles/learning-amp-development /employee-training-and-development-how-to-measure-the-roi-of-training-programs.

Williams, K.B. 2019. "Learner Personas: Beyond Demographics." *TD at Work*, November.

About the Authors

Crystal Kadakia is a two-time TEDx speaker, organizational consultant, and bestselling author known for transforming the toughest workplace changes into exciting possibilities for our digital world. As a consultant, she brings organizations into the digital age, reimagining people strategies with clients in areas such as career development, learning culture, inclusion, leadership development, and employee engagement. Past clients include General Mills, Southern Company, Monster.com, Sierra Club, and other organizations.

Her academic background includes a bachelor's degree in chemical engineering and a master's in organization development. After six years working for Procter & Gamble, she began a consulting firm where she has tackled transforming the status quo and bridging gaps between people in the workplace.

Through her bestselling book, *The Millennial Myth: Transforming Misunderstanding into Workplace Breakthroughs*, and keynotes, Crystal has spent the past decade changing the story for thousands around the generation gap. Along with supporting clients, her next project is a deep study of living and leading in the digital age, including practices that help people create connection, emerge from burnout, and balance the role of technology in our day to day lives.

Crystal is a Power 30 Under 30, CLO Learning in Practice, and ATD One to Watch award recipient. Originally from Austin, Texas, she is now based in Atlanta, Georgia, with her husband, Jeremy, where they love immersing themselves in nature and cultural experiences.

Lisa M.D. Owens is a learning expert who combines her engineering mindset with her deep interest in instructional design and learning sciences to create training that moves business forward.

Following successes in engineering, consumer research, and quality at Procter & Gamble, Lisa was asked to create global training systems. She upskilled with a master's of education and quickly become P&G's top training professional, leading a broad range of cutting-edge internal programs.

After retiring from P&G in 2011, Lisa partnered with Crystal Kadakia to research and solve some of the issues facing L&D in the modern age. This work resulted in a highly rated course on modern learning design. Lisa also co-authored *Leaders as Teachers Action Guide, Your Career: How to Make it Happen*, 9th ed., and *Lo Start-Up Di Una Corporate*

University. Since 2009, she has regularly served as a judge for learning awards, including ATD BEST Awards and CLO ELITE.

Lisa holds a bachelor's degree chemical engineering from Georgia Tech in addition to her MEd. Prior to joining P&G, she cooped at the Savannah River nuclear facility. She is also active in church education and was the lead instructional designer for a nationwide, multiday youth leadership training program. Her youth leadership work continued with her partnership with Helen Chen, founder of China Capable Teens.

In the winter you can find Lisa in Cape Coral, Florida, and she spends warmer months in Ellicott City, Maryland, with her grandchildren. Throughout the year, she and her husband like to travel, with typical destinations being wineries, National Parks, or outdoor and cultural experiences.

Index